Dwayne's Guitar Lessons Presents:
Beginner's Guide to Ukulele Mastery

In Theory and Practice

By
Guitar Teacher
Dwayne Jenkins

Introduction

Welcome to your Beginner's Guide to Ukulele Mastery, a comprehensive resource designed to accompany you on your journey to mastering this vibrant and versatile instrument. No matter if you're a complete beginner or have already taken a few steps.

This guide is divided into sections that allow you to focus on a key aspect of ukulele playing. Begin with the fundamentals, including the history of the ukulele, different types of ukuleles, and tips for choosing the right one for you.

Learn the proper way to hold the ukulele, tune it accurately, and position your hands for optimal playing comfort. Develop your ability to read charts, tablature, and understand timing and rhythm, essential skills for any musician.

Explore common chord progressions, strumming patterns, and dive into major, minor, and pentatonic scales to enhance your musical repertoire. Discover the art of fingerpicking and integrating fingerstyle with strumming to add depth and dynamics to your playing.

Gain a deeper understanding of chord and scale theory, including the relationship between major and relative minor keys. Set goals, develop effective practice habits, and explore strategies to continue your musical journey with enthusiasm and creativity.

The primary aim of this guide is to make learning the ukulele an enjoyable and rewarding experience. By breaking complex concepts into manageable lessons, you'll find it easier to progress at your own pace and celebrate each milestone along the way.

The guide's structured approach ensures that you build a solid foundation before moving on to more advanced techniques. By following this guide, you'll embark on a musical journey filled with discovery and joy.

You'll soon discover that you have something very special in you that you can share and pass on to others. Have patience, practice daily, and above all, have fun—best of luck.

Sincerely, Dwayne Jenkins

Table of Contents

Chapter I: Introduction to the Ukulele

Lesson 1: A Brief History of the Ukulele

The ukulele, a small yet captivating instrument, has a rich history that dates back to the late 19th century. Originating in Hawaii, the ukulele was inspired by several small guitar-like instruments brought to the islands by Portuguese immigrants.

Among these, the most influential were the "machete," "cavaquinho," and "rajão," which were introduced by Madeira Islanders who arrived to work in the sugarcane fields.

The Birth of the Ukulele

The ukulele as we know it today began to take shape around 1879, when three Madeiran cabinetmakers, Manuel Nunes, José do Espírito Santo, and Augusto Dias, began crafting their own versions of the instrument.

Their creative adaptations led to the development of the ukulele's distinct characteristics, such as its re-entrant tuning and its unique, bright sound.

Rise to Popularity

The ukulele quickly gained traction in Hawaiian culture and became an integral part of the islands' musical identity. Playing a pivotal role at royal gatherings and public events further embeds the instrument into the fabric of Hawaiian music.

Global Spread

In the early 20th century, the ukulele's charm spread beyond Hawaii. Its appearance at the Panama-Pacific International Exposition in San Francisco in 1915 introduced the ukulele to the mainland United States, sparking a nationwide fad.

The instrument became synonymous with the Jazz Age and the burgeoning music industry, and its popularity was bolstered by artists and vaudeville performers who embraced its playful, accessible sound.

Modern Relevance

Today, the ukulele continues to resonate with musicians worldwide, celebrated for its simplicity and versatility. It has found a place in various musical genres, from folk and pop to indie and classical, and remains a beloved instrument for beginners and seasoned players alike.

Reflecting on its journey from a humble island creation to a global sensation, the ukulele's enduring appeal lies in its ability to bring joy and connection through music.

With its affordable price and easy portability, it has once again gained popularity. Driven by the digital age of social media, online learning, and the adoption of pop music, it has become a serious instrument to be reckoned with.

Lesson 2: Types of Ukuleles

Explore the diverse world of ukuleles by learning about the different types available and their distinct characteristics. Understanding these variations will help you choose the right instrument for your musical journey.

Soprano Ukulele

The soprano ukulele is the smallest and most traditional size, often considered the "classic" ukulele. It typically measures about 21 inches in length and is known for its bright, cheerful tone.

The soprano ukulele is ideal for beginners due to its compact size, easy portability, and affordable cost. It is the one you see most people play and is often pictured when the ukulele is mentioned.

The Concert Ukulele

Slightly larger than the soprano, the concert ukulele measures approximately 23 inches. It offers a fuller sound and more frets, providing a wider range of notes. The concert ukulele is a great choice for those who find the soprano too small but still want a traditional ukulele sound.

Benefits of the Concert Ukulele

- Comfortable portable size
- A warmer, fuller sound
- For those with bigger hands
- Louder projection

A nice alternative to the soprano ukulele that might be too small or not loud enough.

The Tenor Ukulele

The tenor ukulele is larger, measuring about 26 inches, and features a deeper, richer sound compared to the soprano and concert models.

Its larger body allows for more complex playing techniques, making it popular among professional musicians and those seeking a versatile instrument.

Benefits of the Tenor Ukulele

- Larger body size
- Longer scale length
- Wider fret spacing
- Louder projection
- Ideal for fingerstyle

A great choice for those who choose fingerstyle playing.

The Baritone Ukulele

As the largest of the standard ukulele sizes, the baritone measures around 30 inches. It is tuned differently from the other ukuleles, more closely resembling the tuning of the top four guitar strings.

The baritone produces a deeper, more resonant tone, appealing to players who prefer a richer sound.

Benefits of the Baratone Ukulele

- Deep, rich, warm tone
- Larger body size
- Alternate tuning
- Great for bigger hands

A great way to transition from guitar to the ukulele.

Other Variations

In addition to these standard types, there are other variations such as the sopranissimo (or pocket ukulele), the bass ukulele, and the banjolele, each offering unique sound qualities and playing experiences.

Exploring these options can provide new challenges and opportunities for creative expression.

By familiarizing yourself with these ukulele types, you can make an informed decision when selecting an instrument that matches your personal style and musical goals.

Remember, although there are many different types to choose from, the most common to start with is the soprano ukulele, which is what you see most people playing.

Lesson 3: Choosing the Right One

Selecting the right ukulele is an important step in your musical journey. The right instrument will not only suit your personal taste but also enhance your playing experience. Here are some tips to help you make an informed decision.

Consider Your Skill Level

- **Beginners:** Opt for a soprano or concert ukulele. These sizes are generally easier to handle and more affordable.

An excellent choice for those just starting out.

- **Intermediate and Advanced:** If you're looking to expand your range, consider a tenor or baritone ukulele.

These provide richer tones and an extended note range.

Since this is a guide on beginning your journey with the ukulele, I recommend you start with a soprano. But if that size is too small for your hands, then the concert or tenor.

I recommend avoiding the baritone ukulele, as it is tuned differently, and it's best to learn to play the others first before attempting this one.

Assess the Size

- **Soprano:** Ideal for those who prefer a traditional, bright sound and a lightweight instrument.

Also, a great choice for those with smaller hands and shorter fingers.

- **Concert:** Slightly larger and offers a fuller sound, providing more space on the fretboard.

It is also more ideal for those with slightly larger hands and longer fingers.

Since you're just starting out, I recommend avoiding the baritone ukulele, as it is tuned differently, and it's best to learn to play the others first before attempting this one. You can also choose the tenor, but for our purposes here, we'll focus on the most popular, the soprano.

Examine the Material

- **Wood Types:** The type of wood affects the ukulele's sound. Common woods include mahogany, koa, and spruce.

This is very important to consider once you get good and take the instrument more seriously.

- **Laminate vs. Solid Wood:** Laminate ukuleles are typically more affordable and durable.

Whereas solid wood offers superior sound quality. Solid wood ukuleles will cost more as well.

The size of the ukulele can determine how comfortably it is to play, depending on your body size, especially if you are a bigger person. The material of the instrument can affect the tone quality.

Your Budget

- **Entry-Level Models:** Affordable and great for beginners. A great choice since you're just starting out.

Remember, you don't want to exceed your budget when first starting out.

- **Mid-Range Models:** Offer better sound and build quality.

These are a great choice for when you're getting a bit more serious about the instrument.

- **Professional Models:** Higher quality materials and craftsmanship, suited for serious musicians.

These are excellent for when you're at the level performing on stage or with other serious musicians.

By taking these and other factors into account, you can find a ukulele that not only fits your needs and style but also inspires you to practice more and enjoy the instrument.

Chapter I Quiz

In Chapter 1, we covered the history of the ukulele, types of ukuleles, and choosing which is best for you. This first chapter will lay the foundation for your ukulele-playing journey.

Q: What influenced the development of the ukulelei?
A: ____

Q: What popularized the ukulele in Hawaiian culture?
A: ____

Q: What are the four types of ukuleles you can choose from?
A: ____

Q: What separates the baritone ukulele from the others?
A: ____

Q: Which ukulele is best recommended for beginners?
A: ____

Q: How does the wood type affect the tone of the ukulele?
A: ____

Chapter I Summary

First, you learn that the ukulele, a small yet captivating instrument, has a rich history that dates back to the late 19th century. Originating in Hawaii, the ukulele was inspired by several small guitar-like instruments.

Second, the ukulele as we know it today began to take shape around 1879, when three Madeiran cabinetmakers, Manuel Nunes, José do Espírito Santo, and Augusto Dias, began crafting their own versions of the instrument.

Third, you learn to explore the diverse world of ukuleles by learning about the different types available and their distinct characteristics. Soprano, concert, tenor, and baritone. The baritone is different due to its alternate tuning.

Fourth, selecting the right ukulele is an important step in your musical journey. The right instrument will not only suit your personal taste but also enhance your playing experience.

Lastly, this first chapter is designed to provide an educational foundation for your journey to ukulele proficiency. The stronger your foundation, the better your playing will be.

Chapter II: Getting Started

Lesson 4: Holding the Ukulele

Mastering the proper way to hold your ukulele is essential for comfort and optimal sound production. A correct grip ensures that your playing is both efficient and enjoyable. Here are some tips to help you hold your ukulele with ease:

Positioning Your Body

1. **Sit or Stand Comfortably:** Whether you sit or stand, keep your posture relaxed yet upright.

Your shoulders should be relaxed, and if you're sitting, you should be comfortable.

2. **Align the Ukulele with Your Body:** Hold the ukulele close to your chest, angled slightly upward.

The back of the instrument should rest against your body, with the neck pointing to your left (for right-handed players) or right (for left-handed players).

Supporting the Ukulele

- **Cradle the Body:** Use your right forearm to gently press the body of the ukulele against your chest.

This pressure should be light enough to allow movement but firm enough to keep the instrument steady.

The proper ukulele playing position is crucial to get down, as it will set the tone for everything to come. Creating a solid foundation for playing harmony and melody.

1. **Grip the Neck:** Your left hand should support the neck, with your thumb resting behind it for balance. Avoid gripping too tightly, as this can affect your ability to move freely across the fretboard.

Hand and Arm Placement

1. **Strumming Hand:** Your right hand should hover over the strings near the sound hole.

Use a combination of wrist and forearm movement for strumming, keeping your hand relaxed.

You will need to be able to strum the ukulele with your wrist while it is held with your arm and elbow. This might be awkward at first, but it will become more natural over time.

2. Fretting Hand: Position your fingers parallel to the fretboard and press down on the strings with your fingertips.

Ensure your fingers are curved to allow clean, clear notes without muting adjacent strings.

Notice the hand positioning in the two pictures. The hand is wrapped around the neck, and the fingers are curled, with the strings being played with the fingertips.

Practice Makes Perfect

1. **Experiment with Angles:** Adjust the angle and position
   of the ukulele to find what feels most comfortable for you.

Everyone's body is different, so it may take some time to
discover your ideal hold.

2. **Check for Tension:** Regularly check your body for
   tension, especially in the shoulders and hands.

Relaxing these areas will improve your playing comfort and
sound quality.

By practicing proper holding techniques, you'll set a solid
foundation for your ukulele journey, allowing you to focus on
developing your skills and enjoying the music you create.

Lesson 5: Tuning the Ukulele

Achieving the right sound from your ukulele begins with proper tuning. A well-tuned ukulele not only enhances your playing experience but also ensures that your music is harmonious and pleasing to the ear.

Understanding Standard Tuning

For most ukuleles, the standard tuning is G-C-E-A, from the top string (closest to your face) to the bottom string (closest to your feet). This is commonly called "C tuning" and is used for soprano, concert, and tenor ukuleles.

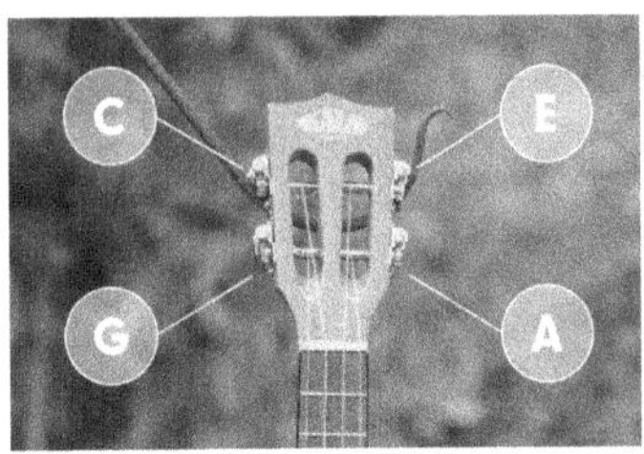

The baritone ukulele, however, is typically tuned to D-G-B-E, like the top four strings of a guitar. For this reason, it is best to start with one of the other three. Find the one that works best for you, and tune it to standard tuning.

Using an Electronic Tuner

1. **Choose Your Tuner:** There are several types of tuners available, including clip-on tuners, smartphone apps, and pedal tuners. Clip-on tuners are particularly convenient for ukulele players, as they attach directly to the headstock.

2. **Turn On the Tuner:** Power on your tuner and set it to the "ukulele" setting if available. If not, the "chromatic" setting will work fine.

3. **Pluck the G String:** Start with the top string (G string). Pluck it gently and watch the tuner display. Adjust the tuning peg until the tuner indicates that the string is in tune.

4. **Tune the C String:** Move to the next string down. Pluck it and adjust the tuning peg as needed to achieve the correct pitch.

5. **Tune the E String:** Repeat the process for the E string, making sure the tuner shows the string is in tune.

6. **Tune the A String:** Finally, pluck the bottom string (A) and adjust as needed.

Tuning Stability and Storage

1. **Check Regularly:** Ukuleles can go out of tune quickly, especially when new strings are installed.

Regularly check your tuning to maintain sound quality. Make sure to use an electronic tuner, as this will give you the best chance for accuracy.

2. **Store Properly:** Temperature and humidity changes can affect tuning.

Store your ukulele in a stable environment to minimize tuning issues. Remember, the ukulele is made of wood, and it can be affected by temperature and climate change.

By learning to tune your ukulele accurately and store it properly, you'll lay the groundwork for creating beautiful music and enjoying a satisfying playing experience.

Lesson 6: Proper Playing Position

Understanding how to position your hands and body while playing the ukulele is crucial for both comfort and efficiency. A good playing posture will help you avoid unnecessary strain and enhance your overall sound quality. Here's how to achieve a proper playing position:

Body and Arm Alignment

1. **Sit or Stand with Good Posture:** Whether seated or standing, maintain an upright but relaxed posture.

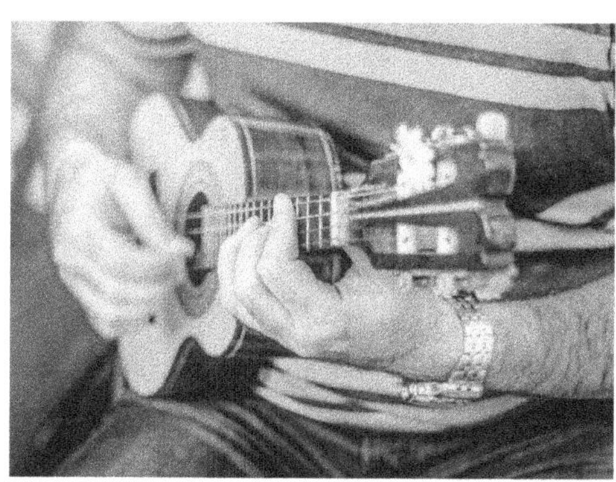

Keep your hands where they can reach the whole instrument.

- **Position the Ukulele:** Hold the ukulele close to your chest with the sound hole facing outward.

The neck should be angled slightly upward, resting comfortably in the crook of your arm.

- **Use Your Right Arm for Support:** Rest your right forearm on the top edge of the ukulele body.

This not only helps stabilize the instrument but also positions your hand for effective strumming or picking.

Hand and Finger Placement

- **Left Hand Positioning:** Your left hand should support the neck of the ukulele. Place your thumb on the back of the neck, roughly opposite your fingers, which will be pressing down on the strings.

Ensure your fingers are curved and press the strings with your fingertips to avoid muting adjacent strings. See previous pictures for details.

- **Right Hand Technique:** For strumming, keep your right hand relaxed and use a smooth wrist motion, not the elbow. Your fingers or a pick should glide over the strings near the sound hole.

For fingerpicking, position your fingers over the strings and pluck with your thumb and fingers. See previous pictures for details.

Finding Your Comfort Zone

1. **Experiment with Angles and Positions:** Adjust the ukulele's angle and position to find what feels most comfortable.

Everyone's physique is different, so it's important to find a position that works for you.

- **Ease Tension:** Regularly check for tension in your shoulders, arms, and hands.

Relaxation is key to smooth playing and preventing fatigue or injury.

Here are a couple of examples of what your playing position should look like. Sitting or standing.

Chapter II Quiz

In Chapter 2, you have learned about the proper way to hold the ukulele, the proper way to tune the ukulele, and proper hand positioning. All very important factors in getting started.

Q: Why is it important to learn to hold the ukulele properly?
A: ____

Q: What is the ideal forearm position for holding the ukulele?
A: ____

Q: What is the standard tuning for most ukuleles?
A: ____

Q: Why is it beneficial to use an electronic tuner for tuning?
A: ____

Q: What is it beneficial to maintain a relaxed posture?
A: ____

Q: What is the best positioning for the fretboard hand?
A: ____

*Remember, all the answers can be found within the lessons of the chapters.

Chapter II Summary

<u>First</u>, you learn that selecting the right ukulele is an important step in your musical journey. The right instrument will not only suit your personal taste but also enhance your playing experience.

<u>Second</u>, you learn that since you're just starting out, it is recommended to avoid the baritone ukulele. It is tuned differently, and it's best to learn to play the others first before attempting this one.

<u>Third</u>, you learn that achieving the right sound from your ukulele begins with proper tuning. A well-tuned ukulele not only enhances your playing experience but also ensures that your music is harmonious.

<u>Fourth</u>, you learned that understanding how to position your hands and body while playing the ukulele is crucial for both comfort and efficiency. A good playing posture will help you avoid unnecessary strain and enhance your sound quality.

<u>Lastly</u>, by choosing the ukulele that's right for you, learning to tune it properly, and focusing on proper playing positions, you set yourself up for future success.

Chapter III: Reading Ukulele Notation

Lesson 7: Charts and Scale Diagrams

Understanding charts and scale diagrams is a fundamental aspect of learning to play the ukulele. These visual tools help you identify finger placements, comprehend scales, and navigate the fretboard efficiently.

 Mastering these concepts will enhance your ability to read music and improve your overall musicianship.

Understanding Ukulele Charts

Ukulele charts, often referred to as chord charts, display the finger positions required to play specific chords. They are comprised of vertical and horizontal lines within a box diagram.

These give you a quick visual reference guide for which frets and strings to play on. These are also very popular with other stringed instruments, such as the guitar. So by learning to read them, you enhance your musicianship.

Ukulele Chord Chart

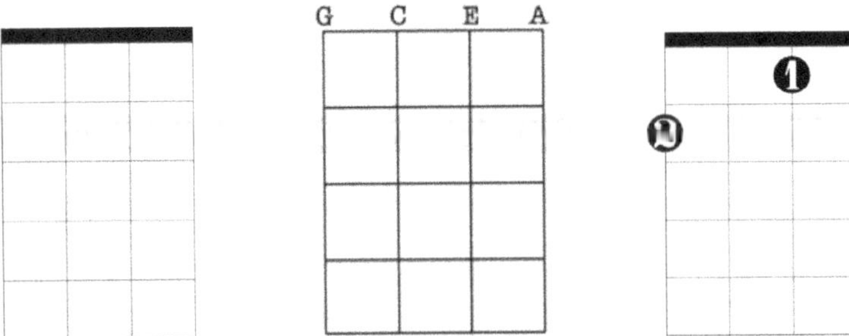

- **Vertical Lines:** These represent the strings of the ukulele. From left to right, they correspond to the G, C, E, and A strings.
- **Horizontal Lines:** These lines denote the frets. The top horizontal line usually represents the nut (the top of the fretboard), while the lines below indicate subsequent frets.
- **Dots:** Placed on these lines, dots show where to press down on the strings. Each dot corresponds to a finger placement on the fretboard.
- **Numbers:** Sometimes, numbers are placed above the dots to indicate which fingers to use. For example, 1 for the index finger, 2 for the middle finger, etc.

Scale Diagrams

Scale diagrams are similar to charts, but they are used to read scales. They can be presented horizontally or vertically. For our purposes here, we'll look at them vertically.

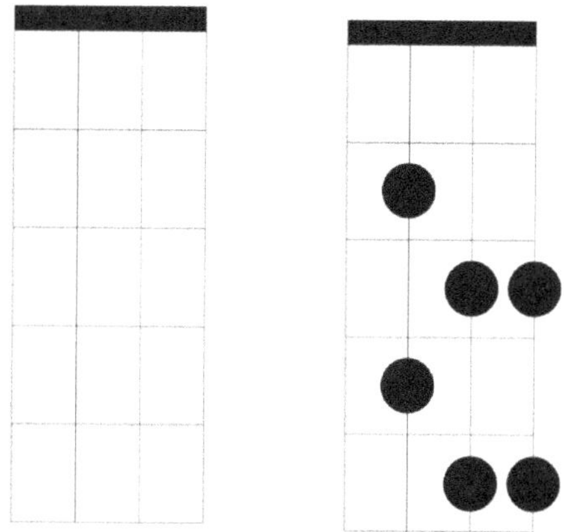

- **Vertical Diagram:** This is just like the chord chart. Strings are the vertical lines, and frets are the horizontal ones.
- **Finger placement:** Like chord charts, you will use dots to indicate finger placement along the frets.

Applying Charts and Diagrams

- **Chord Charts:** These can be used to communicate a song's structure without the need to read full notation.

This also allows you to learn songs faster and get ideas for your own song construction.

- **Scale Diagrams:** These give you a bird's eye view of scale note patterns, enabling faster learning.

Also, allowing for quicker memorization and better fretboard navigation. Allowing you to enhance your improvisation.

- **Understanding Musical Context:** Use charts and diagrams to analyze songs and understand their musical structure.

This will deepen your musical comprehension and aid in songwriting. By mastering charts and scale diagrams, you'll gain a solid foundation in navigating the ukulele fretboard, allowing you to explore more complex musical pieces and express yourself creatively.

Lesson 8: Reading Ukulele Tablature

Understanding how to read ukulele tablature (or tabs) is a crucial skill for any player, as it provides a simple and effective way to learn songs without needing to read traditional music notation.

Tablature is a visual representation of the ukulele's fretboard and indicates where to place your fingers to play specific notes. Here's how to decipher ukulele tabs and some tips to get you started:

Basics of Ukulele Tabs

- **Tab Structure:** Ukulele tabs consist of four horizontal lines, each representing a ukulele string. From top to bottom, the lines correspond to the A, E, C, and G strings, reflecting the standard tuning of the ukulele.

***Remember, the strings will be reversed in the sheet music.**

- **Fret Numbers:** Numbers are written on the lines to indicate which fret to press on that string. For example, a "3" on the top line means you press the third fret on the A string.

- **Reading Direction:** Tabs are read from left to right, like a book. The sequence of numbers indicates the order in which notes should be played.

In this example, you will play the notes one at a time. Start on the 3rd fret of the A string and proceed to the 5th fret on the E string.

Techniques and Symbols

- **Chords:** When numbers are stacked vertically, they represent a chord. Play all the indicated frets simultaneously.

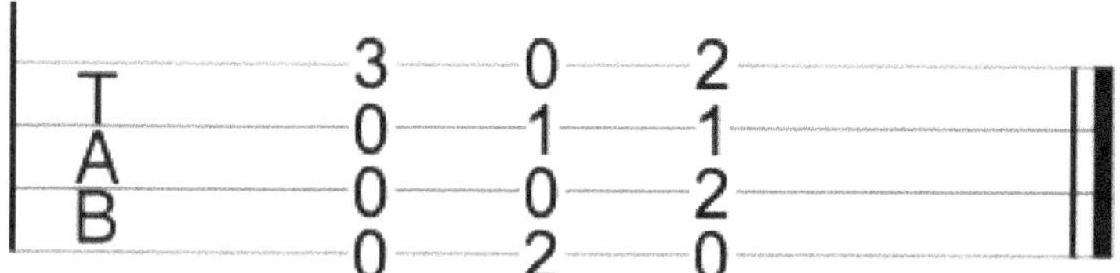

In this example, you have the C major, F major, and G7 chords.

- **Hammer-ons and Pull-offs:** Often noted by an arc for both hammer-ons and pull-offs between two notes. They will be differentiated by an H and a P over the arc.

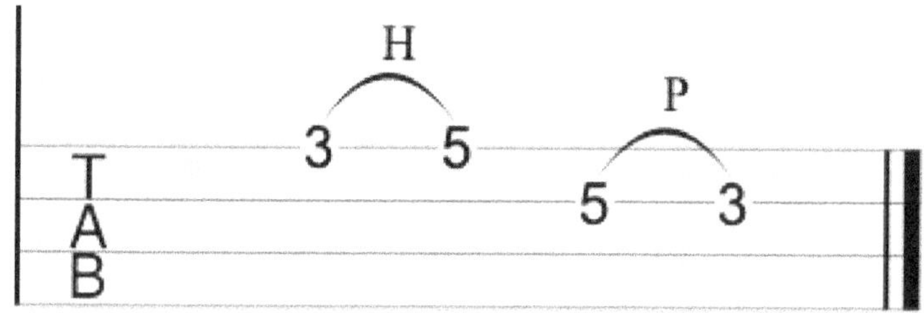

Here, you hammer-on to the 5th fret from the 3rd, on the A string, and do a pull-off from the 5th to the 3rd on the E string.

- **Slides:** Represented by a slash ("/" for sliding up, "\"
  for sliding down). For example, "5/7" means slide up
  from the 5th fret to the 7th fret, and "7\5" means
  slide down.

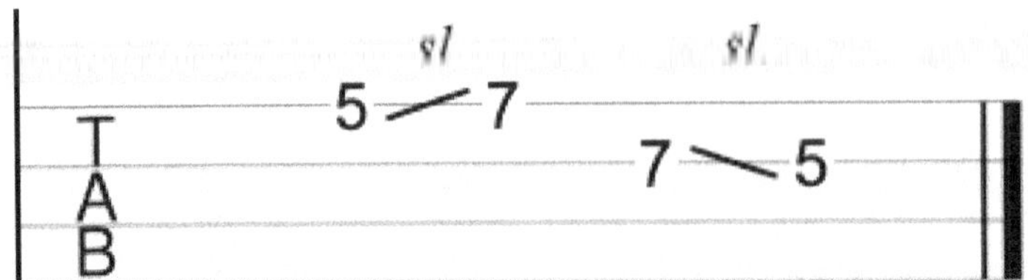

In this example, you use the A and E strings for sliding up and
down at the 5th and 7th frets.

- **Bends:** Indicated by an arrow facing upward,
  instructing you to bend the string at the specified
  fret to reach a higher pitch.

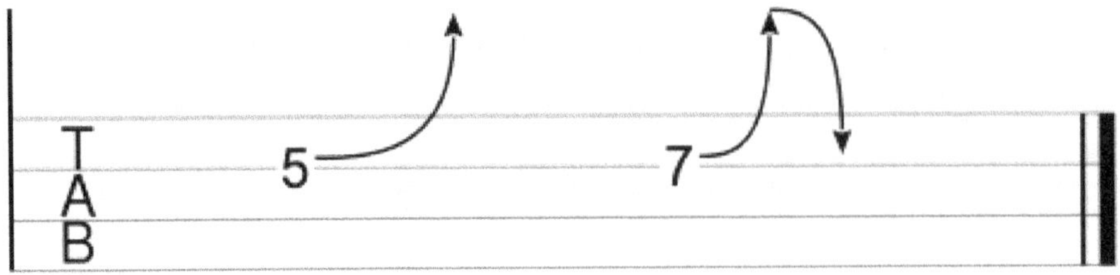

In these two examples, you have a bend at the 5th fret on the E
string, and then an example of a bend release at the 5th fret on
the E string.

- **Vibrato:** Indicated by a squiggly line above the fret that is being vibrated.

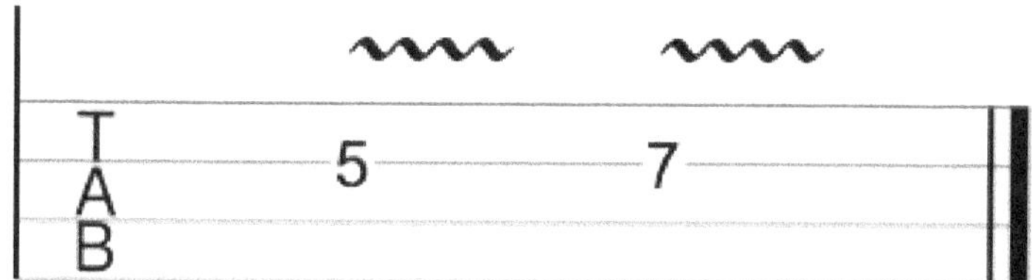

In this example, you have vibrato at the 5th nd 7th frets on the A string. This is done by gently vibrating the note up and down.

- **Trills:** These are repeated hammer-ons and pull-offs performed quickly. Indicated by a tr and squiggly line above the first note.

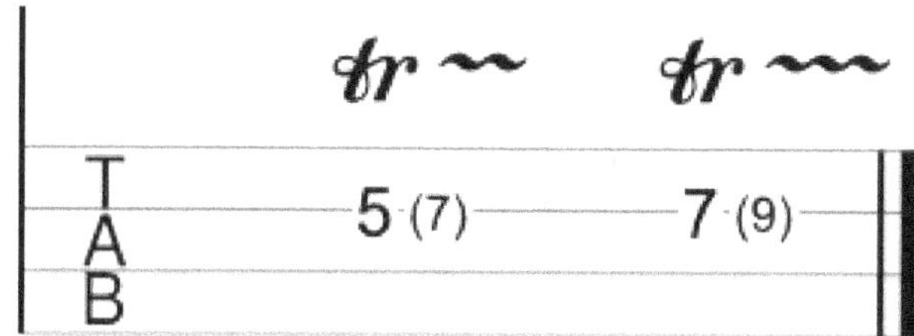

In this example, you play trills on the 5th and 7th frets on the A string. These give the notes an exciting expression.

*Study and practice these daily for optimum performance.

Ukulele Tab Practice Tips

- **Start Simple:** Begin with simple songs or riffs to familiarize yourself with tab structure and basic finger placement.

This will help you to become comfortable with reading tabs and referring them to the fretboard.

- **Slow It Down:** Practice slowly to ensure accuracy, then gradually increase speed as you become more comfortable with the tablature.

Break it down into sections for easier learning and a better understanding of the song structure.

- **Combine Listening and Reading:** Listen to the song while following along with the tab to understand the rhythm and timing.

By mastering ukulele tablature, you'll unlock a vast array of music to explore and enjoy, enhancing your ability to learn and perform songs with ease.

Lesson 9: Timing and Rhythm

Mastering timing and rhythm is fundamental to any musician's development, including ukulele players. These skills ensure that your music flows smoothly and that you can play in sync with others or along with backing tracks.

Understanding Rhythm

Beat and Tempo: The beat is the basic unit of time in music, and tempo refers to the speed of the beat.

Practice clapping or tapping along with a metronome to grasp the steady pulse of a song.

Time Signatures: Familiarize yourself with common time signatures, such as 4/4, 2/4, and 3/4 timing.

The top number indicates how many beats are in a measure, while the bottom number indicates the note value.

Rhythmic Patterns: Learn to recognize and play various rhythmic patterns, using quarter notes, eighth notes, and triplets. Practice these patterns through strumming exercises or using simple songs.

Techniques to Improve Timing

1. **Use a Metronome:** An invaluable tool for developing consistent timing.

Start at a slow tempo and gradually increase the speed as you become more comfortable.

2. **Count Aloud:** Counting aloud while playing helps internalize the rhythm.

For example, in 4/4 time, count "1, 2, 3, 4" to stay on track.

3. **Subdivision Practice:** Break down each beat into smaller subdivisions.

Practice playing quarter notes, eighth notes, and triplets.

- **Identifying Riffs in Music**: Listen to various songs to identify their riffs. Pay attention to the rhythm, melody, and repetition that characterize each riff. Understanding these elements will help you recognize and learn riffs more efficiently.

Exercises to Enhance Rhythm

1. **Clap and Tap:** Clap or tap out rhythms before playing them on the ukulele.

This helps you focus solely on the rhythm without worrying about finger placement.

2. **Strumming Patterns:** Experiment with different strumming patterns, such as down-up strokes, to diversify your playing style.

Practice these patterns and then incorporate them into songs.

3. **Play Along with Recordings:** Use recordings of songs or backing tracks to practice playing in time with other musicians.

This will help you develop the ability to lock into a groove and enhance your rhythmic feel.

By focusing on timing and rhythm, you'll improve your musicality, enabling you to play more confidently and cohesively, whether solo or with others.

Common Timing Sequences

- **Quarter Notes:** These are equal to one beat, and in common time (4/4), you play four beats per measure

These will count as: **1 2 3 4.**

- **Eighth Notes**: These are two notes tied together and are played twice as fast in common time.

These will count as: **1 & 2 & 3 & 4 &.**

- **Triplets**: These are three notes tied together, played in the time of one quarter note, and provide a unique rhythm sequence.

These will count as: **1 & uh, 2 & uh, 3 & uh, 4 & uh.**

- **Triplets**: These are four notes tied together and will equal an even faster timing sequence.

These will count as: **1 e & uh, 2 e & uh, 3 e & uh, 4 e & uh.**

Most rhythms will be made up of these timing sequences. Usually, a standalone timing or a mixture. Practice these timing sequences, and learn how they affect the rhythm.

Chapter III Quiz

In Chapter 3, you have learned about reading ukulele notation. Chord charts, scale diagrams, tablature, and building rhythm and timing. All are important for enhancing your musicianship.

Q: What do the vertical lines represent in ukulele chord charts?
A: ____

Q: What does a dot represent when reading a scale diagram?
A: ____

Q: When reading ukulele tabs, what do the numbers indicate?
A: ____

Q: What does it mean in tabs when numbers are stacked?
A: ____

Q: What role does the metronome play in developing timing?
A: ____

Q: In 4/4 time, how many beats are in a measure?
A: ____

*Look for the answers inside the lessons in the chapter.

Chapter III summary

<u>First</u>, you learn that understanding charts and scale diagrams is a fundamental aspect of learning to play the ukulele. They help you to identify finger placements, comprehend scales, and navigate the fretboard efficiently.

<u>Second</u>, you learn that Ukulele charts, often referred to as chord charts, display the finger positions required to play specific chords. They are comprised of vertical and horizontal lines within a box diagram.

<u>Third</u>, you learn that Scale diagrams are similar to charts, but they are used to read scales. They can be presented horizontally or vertically, and can help you to quickly navigate the ukulele fretboard.

<u>Fourth</u>, you learn that understanding how to read ukulele tablature (or tabs) is a crucial skill for any player, as it provides a simple and effective way to learn songs without needing to read traditional music notation.

<u>Lastly</u>, mastering timing and rhythm is fundamental to any musician's development, including ukulele players. These skills ensure that your music flows smoothly and that you can play in sync with others or along with backing tracks.

Chapter IV: Playing Ukulele Chords

Lesson 10: Common Chords Found in Songs

Learning common ukulele chords is a key step toward playing a wide variety of songs. These chords form the backbone of many popular tunes, and mastering them will enable you to accompany yourself or others effectively.

Here's a guide to some of the most frequently used ukulele chords:

Essential Chords for Beginners

- **C Major (C):**

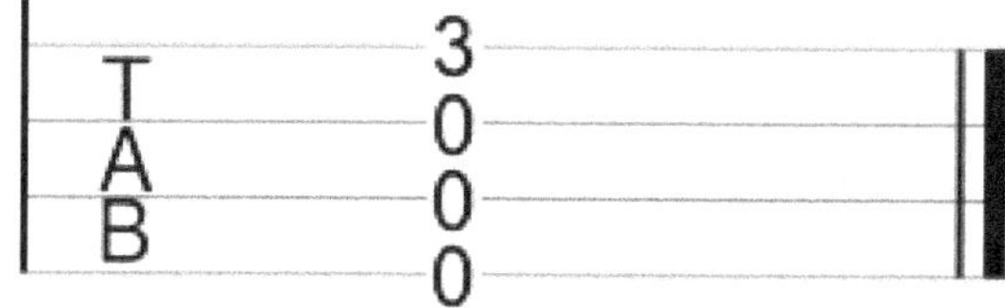

Place your ring finger on the 3rd fret of the A string. Allow the other strings to ring open.

- **F Major (F):**

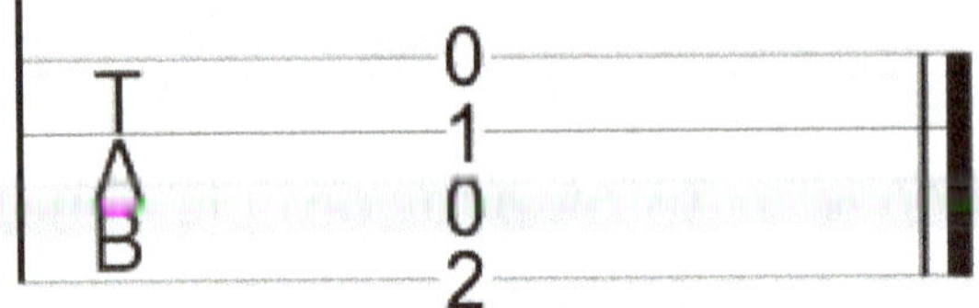

Place your index finger on the 1st fret of the E string. Place your middle finger on the 2nd fret of the G string.

- **G Seven (G7):**

Place your index finger on the 2nd fret of the C string. Place your middle finger on the 2nd fret of the A string. Place your ring finger on the 1st fret of the E string.

- G7 is presented before G major because it is a more natural transition from F major. There are many ukulele songs that can be played with C, F, & G7.

- **A Minor (Am):**

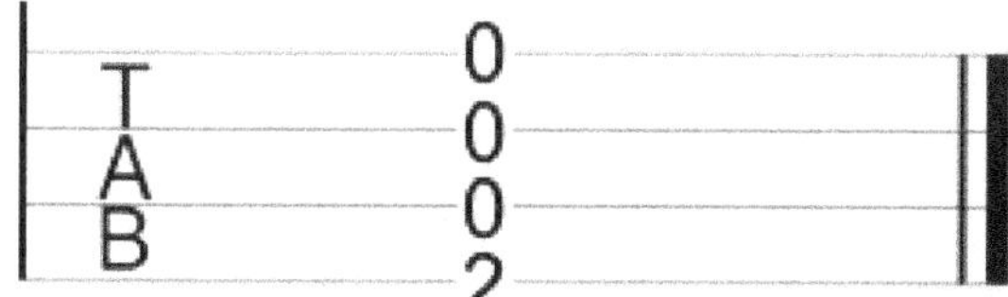

Place your middle finger on the 2nd fret of the G string. Leave the other strings open.

- **E Minor (Em):**

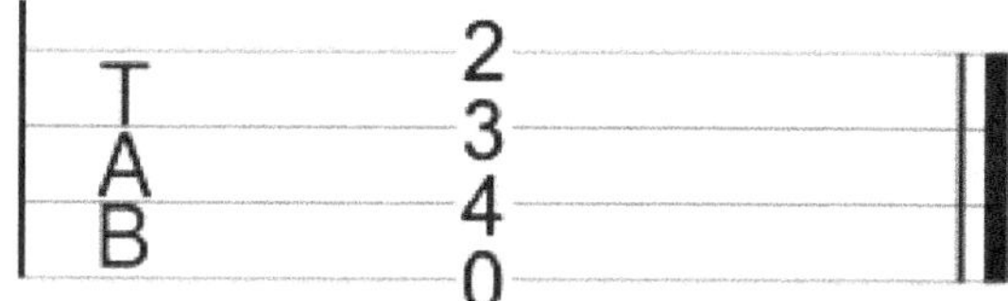

Place your index finger on the 2nd fret of the A string, your middle finger on the 3rd fret of the E string, your ring finger on the 4th fret of the C string, and play the G string open.

These two minor chords are the most common in songs, so make sure you study and practice them daily.

- **G Major (G):**

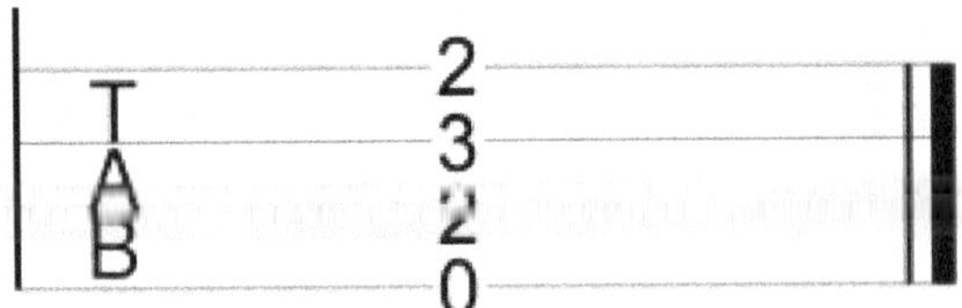

Place your index finger on the 2nd fret of the C string. Place your middle finger on the 2nd fret of the A string. Place your ring finger on the 3rd fret of the E string.

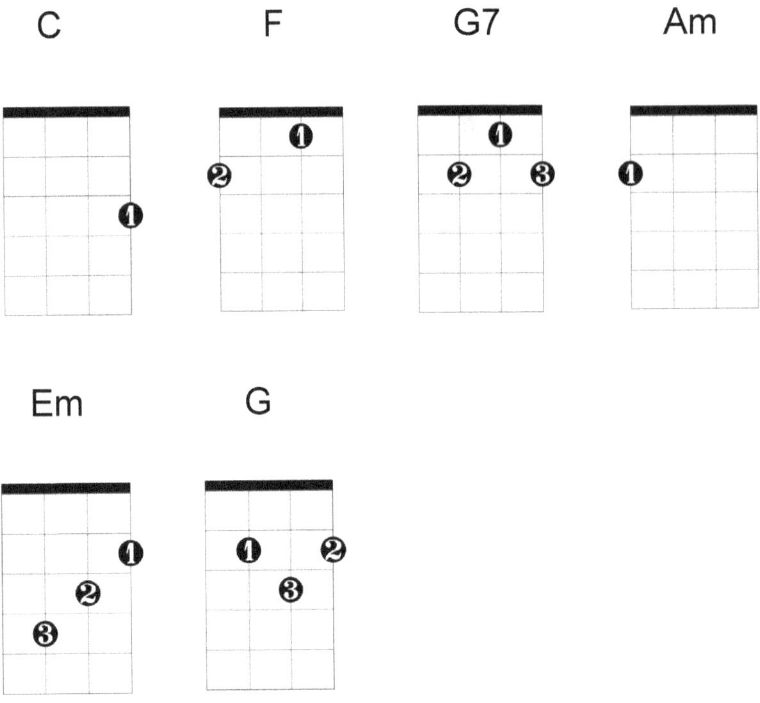

Switching Between Chords

Once you're comfortable with these basic chords, practice switching between them to build dexterity and fluidity in your hands and fingers. Here are a few exercises to get you started:

- **C - F - C - F:** These two chords are in many songs and commonly transition between each other.

I recommend you practice these two first.

- **F - G7 - F - G7:** These are also found in many songs, transitioning between each other like the C and F.

Practice switching between these two chords next.

- **G7 - C - G7 - C:** These two will be the easiest when you get to this point, as they are right next to each other.

These three chords are very common in many songs and will serve you well to start out with. Once you get these down, add the other chords you've learned. Remember, switching between chords is the foundation of songs.

Practice Tips

- **Smooth Transitions:** Practice moving from one chord to another smoothly and without pause, just like I presented earlier in this lesson.

This will help you play songs more smoothly once you reach that level.

- **Strumming Patterns:** Experiment with different strumming patterns to add variety to your playing.

Strumming patterns will be presented in the next lesson to help with this training tip.

- **Play Along:** Use backing tracks or play along with recordings to practice keeping time and staying in rhythm.

By mastering these common chords and experimenting with different exercises for development, you'll gain the confidence and ability to play a wide range of songs, laying a solid foundation for your musical journey with the ukulele.

Lesson 11: Creating Chord Progressions

After learning to switch chords, you want to work on creating chord progressions. These are fundamental skills for any musician, as it forms the structure and foundation of a song.

By understanding how to construct and experiment with chord progressions, you'll be able to compose your own music and enhance your playing experience on the ukulele.

Understanding Chord Progressions

- **Basic Definition:** A chord progression is a sequence of chords played in a particular order.

It creates a sense of movement and emotional direction in a piece of music.

- **Common Progressions:** Familiarize yourself with common progressions.

Such as I-IV-V and II-V-I, which are widely used across many musical genres.

Building Your Own Progressions

1. **Identify the Key:** Start by deciding the key of your song. This will determine the chords available to you.

For example, In the key of C major, the primary chords are C, F, and G.

2. **Select Chords:** Choose chords that fit within the key to add emotion and diversity.

Experiment with major, minor, and seventh chords to create different moods and textures.

3. **Experiment with Order:** Play around with the order of the chords. Changing the sequence can dramatically alter the music's feel.

This is the art of songwriting, controlling the emotion of what you're trying to convey.

Mastering these fundamental principles will give you a solid foundation for learning your favorite songs and creating your own magical musical landscapes.

12-Bar Chord Progression in C Major

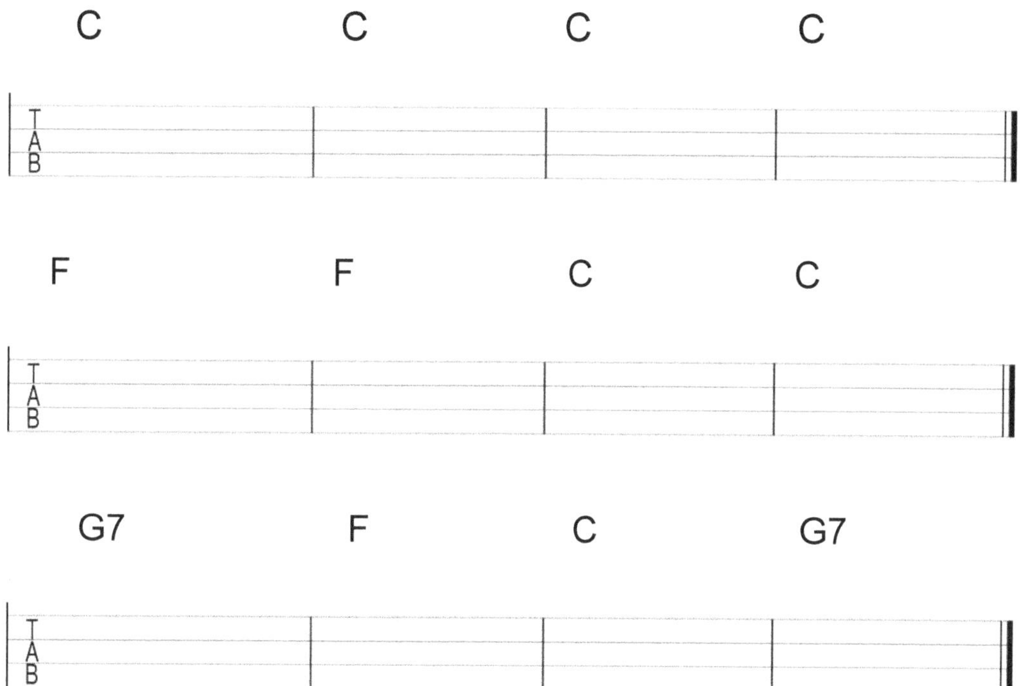

This is the most common chord progression in music, consisting of three chords. The I-IV-V. In this example, we'll use the G7 for easier chord transition. Also, try this with the other progression mentioned in this lesson, the II-V-I, and compare the sound of the two.

C Major: **C D E F G A B** = 1 2 3 4 5 6 7

Notice how the chord progression is created over twelve bars of music. This is why it is called the 12-bar progression. It is commonly found in many popular songs in multiple genres.

The I, IV, and V chords in any key can be used to create this progression.

Other Keys Commonly Used For Chord Progressions

G Major: G A B C D E F = 1 2 3 4 5 6 7

A Minor: A B C D E F G = 1 2 b3 4 5 b6 b7

E Minor: E F# G A B C D = 1 2 b3 4 5 b6 b7

D Major: D E F# G A B C# = 1 2 3 4 5 6 7

When you play a major key, all notes are in their natural place. That's why the major key produces a happy sound. When you flatten a few notes in the major key to create the minor key, it gives the minor key a sad, somber sound.

This is how you control emotion in your music. Get familiar with these keys and the notes they contain.

Tips for Creating Interesting Progressions

1. **Incorporate Tension and Release:** Use tension-building chords (such as dominant sevenths) followed by resolution (such as the tonic chord) to create a satisfying musical journey.

This will help control the music's dynamics. Remember, music is all about emotion.

2. **Add Variations:** Introduce chord inversions or substitute chords to add interest and complexity.

Chords have a wide variety of applications when used in this manner, so make sure to take advantage of them.

3. **Explore Rhythm:** Vary the rhythm of your chord changes. Syncopation or unexpected timing can add a unique flair to your progression.

This approach to timing alterations hits the listener's ear at a different angle and grabs their attention.

Practice and Application

1. **Journaling Progressions:** Keep a journal of your favorite chord progressions.

This can serve as a resource for future songwriting projects.

2. **Listen and Analyze:** Listen to songs you love and analyze their chord progressions.

Understanding how others use progressions can inspire your own creations.

3. **Compose and Share:** Use your progressions to compose original pieces or to accompany existing melodies.

Share your creations with others to gain feedback and further your skills.

By mastering the art of creating chord progressions, you'll enhance your ability to compose music and express your individual creativity on the ukulele.

Lesson 12: Strumming with Chords

Strumming is an essential skill for ukulele players, as it brings rhythm and texture to your music. By effectively combining strumming with chords, you can enhance your performance and add depth to your playing. Here are some tips and techniques to help you strum with confidence and style:

Understanding Strumming Basics

- **Grip and Position:** Hold the ukulele comfortably with your right arm resting on the body and your right hand positioned over the sound hole.

Use a loose grip on your pick (if using one) or keep your strumming fingers relaxed.

- **Strumming Motion:** Use a relaxed wrist motion to strum, rather than moving your entire arm.

This allows for smooth, controlled arm movement while strumming.

- **Consistency:** Maintain a steady tempo as you strum. Start with simple downstrokes to get a feel for the rhythm.

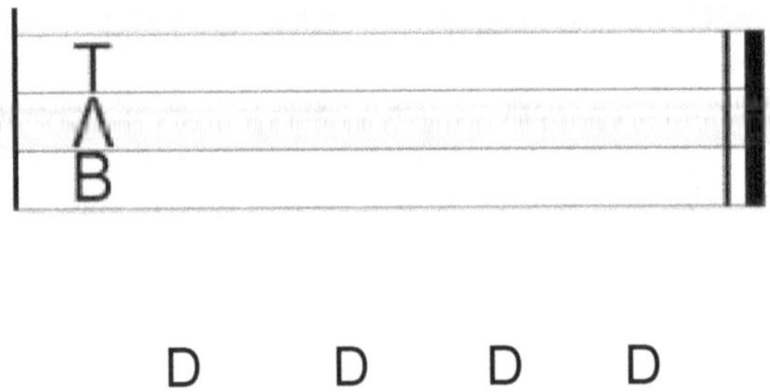

Exploring Strumming Patterns

1. **Down-Up Strumming:** Begin with a basic down-up pattern.

Strum down on the beat and up in between beats. Practice this pattern slowly, gradually increasing your speed.

2. **Emphasizing Beats:** Add emphasis to certain beats by strumming harder or accentuating specific downstrokes. This can create a more dynamic feel.

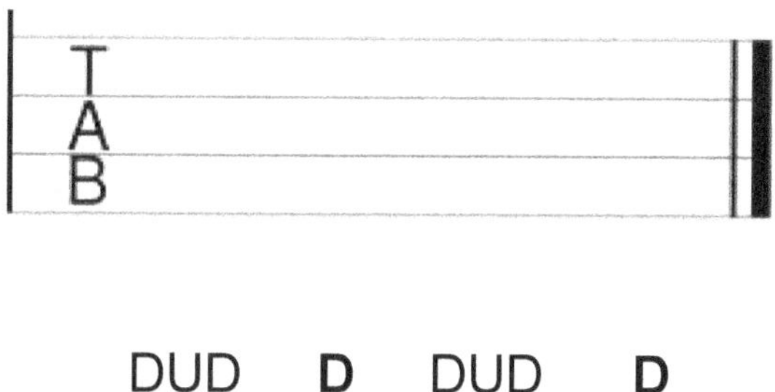

DUD **D** DUD **D**

3. **Syncopation:** Experiment with syncopated patterns by varying the timing of your strums.

1 2 3 & 4

This is where the different timing sequences you learned earlier come into play. They can add interest and complexity to your musical landscapes. Mix up your quarter notes, eighth notes, triplets, and sixteenth notes to get this effect.

Techniques to Enhance Your Strumming

1. **Muting:** Use the palm of your strumming hand to lightly mute the strings after a strum.

This technique can create a percussive effect and add rhythm to your music.

2. **Percussion:** Incorporate "percussion" by lightly pressing down on the strings with your strumming hand immediately after a strum.

This technique produces a muted, percussive sound, very common on stringed instruments.

3. **Strumming Variations:** Try different strumming patterns to diversify your sound. The calypso strum typically follows a "down, down-up, up-down-up" pattern.

D   DU   UDU

Additional Strumming Patterns

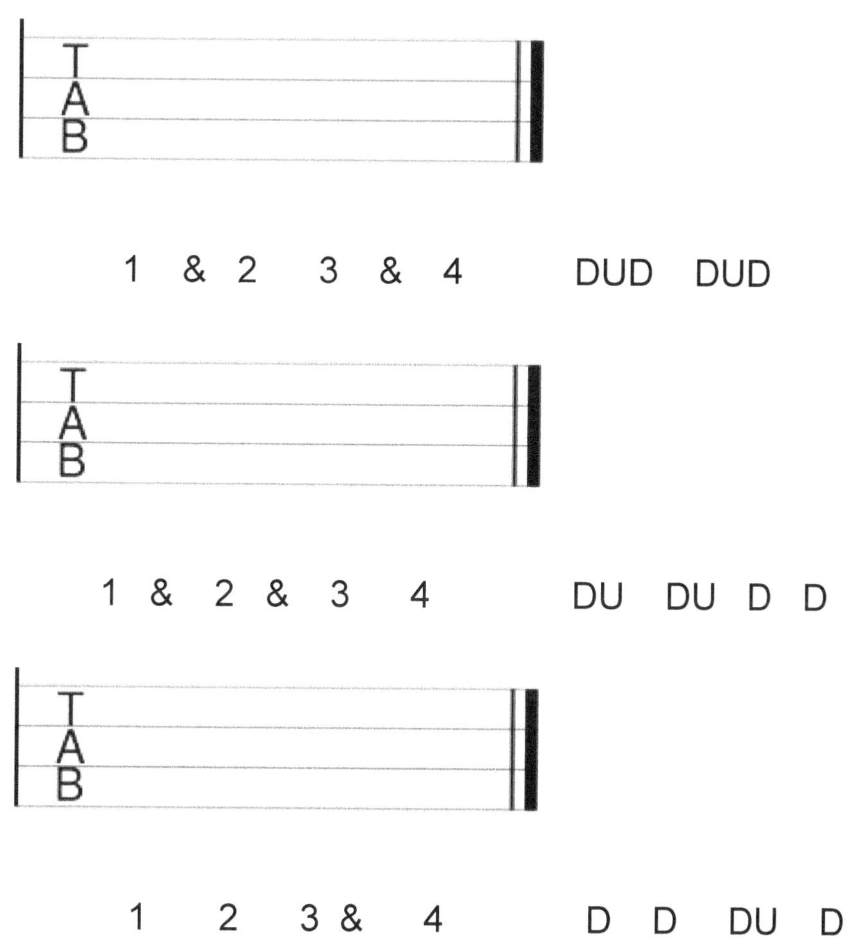

These will help you to develop your strumming, timing, and rhythm. Practice them daily, and create your own variations.

Practice Tips

1. **Use a Metronome:** Practice strumming along with a metronome.

This approach will help you develop a consistent rhythm and improve your timing.

2. **Combine with Chords:** Practice transitioning between chords while maintaining your strumming pattern.

Start slowly and focus on smooth transitions. Make sure to get the chords down before incorporating strumming.

3. **Listen and Learn:** Listen to recordings of ukulele players to understand how they incorporate strumming into their music.

By analyzing their techniques and trying to replicate them, you get a better understanding of how these concepts work together in songs.

By mastering strumming with chords, you'll be able to play a wide variety of songs and develop your unique playing style.

Chapter IV Quiz

In Chapter 4, you learn about common chords found in songs, creating chord progressions, and how to strum with chords. All essential techniques for playing rhythm.

Q: What is the chord you should learn first on the ukulele?

A: ____

Q: How is the G7 chord different from the G major chord?

A: ____

Q: What is the most common progression in many genres?

A: ____

Q: What is the first step in creating your own progressions?

A: ____

Q: What helps maintain a consistent strumming pattern?

A: ____

Q: What pattern is commonly used in the calypso strum?

A: ____

*If you don't know the answer, go back through the lesson.

Chapter IV Summary

<u>First</u>, learning common ukulele chords is a key step toward playing a wide variety of songs. These chords form the backbone of many popular tunes, and mastering them will enable you to accompany yourself or others effectively.

<u>Second</u>, you learn the C major, F major, G7, A minor, E minor, and G major. Six chords that are commonly found in many, many songs, and will make up the foundation of your chord vocabulary.

<u>Third</u>, you learn that by understanding how to construct and experiment with chord progressions, you'll be able to compose your own music and enhance your playing experience on the ukulele.

<u>Fourth</u>, you learn that Strumming is an essential skill for ukulele players, as it brings rhythm and texture to your music. By effectively combining strumming with chords, you can enhance your performance.

<u>Lastly</u>, by learning common chords, chord progressions, and how to strum with them, you will build a solid foundation for playing rhythm on the ukulele.

Chapter V: Playing Scales

Lesson 13: Developing Finger Dexterity

Developing finger dexterity is crucial for ukulele players who want to play with precision and fluidity. This skill allows you to navigate the fretboard and perform intricate melodies.

Warm-Up Exercises

- **One Finger Per Fret:** Begin with a simple finger per fret exercise. Allowing you to build dexterity in all four fingers.

- **Spider Walk:** Place your fingers on the fretboard as if they were "walking" across the strings.

Repeat these exercises several times to increase flexibility and mobility in your fingers, ensuring each note rings clearly. This will allow you to develop independence in your fingers.

66

More Finger Exercises

1. Finger Reverse: Start with the first finger and jump to the third, then proceed with the second and fourth.

Repeat this, starting with a different finger each time.

Open Strings: Start out with open strings as you progress throughout the exercise.

Move to the next string and alter the pattern. This exercise helps coordinate finger movements and build speed.

Using open strings and changing up the order allows different fingers to lead the exercise. This helps with muscle memory and eye-hand coordination.

*Be sure to practice these daily for the best results.

Improving Coordination

1. **Finger Independence:** Practice lifting and placing each finger independently while maintaining the others in position.

Focus on clarity and precision, ensuring that each note is distinct.

2. **Chord Changes:** Choose two chords and practice transitioning between them smoothly.

Start slowly, focusing on accuracy, and gradually increase your speed as you become more comfortable.

Improving your coordination is highly important. By focusing on proper finger placement, you'll produce a much cleaner sound. By focusing on simple two-chord changes, you'll prepare yourself for playing simple songs.

Remember, many popular songs can be played with just three chords. The more you exercise your fingers, the better your playing will sound.

Tips for Effective Practice

1. **Use a Metronome:** Start at a slow tempo and gradually increase it as you gain confidence.

This helps develop timing and consistency.

2. **Focus on Relaxation:** Avoid tension in your hands and arms.

Keep movements fluid and relaxed to prevent strain.

3. **Regular Practice:** Dedicate a few minutes each day to finger exercises.

Consistent practice is key to developing lasting dexterity.

By incorporating these exercises into your practice routine, you'll improve your finger dexterity, enabling you to play more complex pieces and express yourself more fully on the ukulele. This foundational skill will significantly enhance your overall musicianship.

Lesson 14: Major and Minor Scales

Understanding major and minor scales is essential for any ukulele player looking to expand their musical knowledge and enhance their playing skills. These scales form the foundation of Western music and are crucial for improvisation, songwriting, and understanding chord progressions.

Here's a guide to help you learn and practice major and minor scales on the ukulele:

Major Scales

Structure of the Major Scale

1. **Whole and Half Steps:** The major scale consists of a specific pattern of whole steps (W) and half steps (H): W-W-H-W-W-W-H.

C Major Scale: C-w-D-w-E-h-F-w-G-w-A-w-B-h-C

This pattern works across all major scales, no matter what major key you choose to play in. Master the formula, and you will master the notes of any major scale.

2. C Major Example: The C major scale on the ukulele, starting from the open C string, follows this pattern:

This same pattern works with the other major scales, starting with the open strings.

G Major Scale: G A B C D E F# G

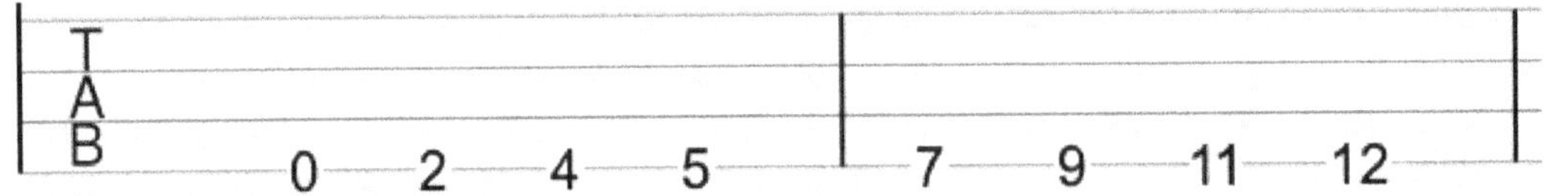

E Major Scale: E F# G# A B C# D# E

A Major Scale: A B C# D E F# G# A

Practicing Major Scales

- **Fretboard Navigation:** Start with the C major scale and practice ascending and descending the fretboard.

Focus on clean transitions between notes and where you are located on the fretboard.

- **Finger Positioning:** Use one finger per fret to ensure smooth and efficient movement.

This is where the finger exercises that were presented earlier come in handy.

- **Speed and Accuracy:** Begin slowly to ensure accuracy, then gradually increase your speed as you become more comfortable.

This will help you master note accuracy along the fretboard.

Fretboard navigation, finger positioning, and speed accuracy will help you to master the major scale and enhance your overall musicianship.

Minor Scales

Structure of the Minor Scale

1. Natural Minor Scale: The natural minor scale follows its own pattern of whole and half steps: W-H-W-W-H-W-W.

A Minor Scale: A-w-B-h-C-w-D-w-E-h-F-w-G-w-A

The minor scale flattens the 3rd, 6th, and 7th of the major.

2. A & E Minor Examples: The A & E natural minor scales, starting from the open strings, are as follows

```
         0   2   3   5       7   8   10   12
T
A
B
```

This works with the other minor scales as well, just like with the major scale. Just flatten the 3rd, 6th, and 7th notes.

E minor Scale: E F# G A B C D E

```
T        0   2   3   5       7   8   10   12
A
B
```

Practicing Minor Scales

- **Consistency in Practice:** Just like with major scales, practice the A minor scale regularly, focusing on both precision and fluidity.

Take note how A minor is made up of the same notes as C major.

- **Compare and Contrast:** Notice the difference in sound between major and minor scales—major scales typically sound brighter, while minor scales have a more somber tone.

This is a great way to add emotion to the musical journey you take your listeners on.

Develop consistency in practice, and work with using both major and minor scales. This will expand your musicianship and deepen your understanding of these two fundamental scales across multiple keys.

Applications of Scales

1. **Improvisation:** Use scales as a basis for creating melodies and solos.

Experiment with combining notes from the scales to develop your unique musical ideas.

2. **Songwriting:** Understanding scales helps in crafting chord progressions and melodies.

Enabling you to write songs with depth and control the emotion of your musical compositions.

3. **Musical Analysis:** Analyze songs to identify the scales that are used.

This will enhance your understanding of their structure and harmony.

By mastering major and minor scales, you'll gain a deeper understanding of music theory and increase your versatility as a ukulele player.

Lesson 15: The Pentatonic Scale

The pentatonic scales are a powerful tool for ukulele players, offering a simplified yet versatile approach to improvisation and melody creation. These five-note scales are prevalent in numerous musical genres, including blues, rock, pop, and folk.

Understanding and mastering pentatonic scales can significantly enhance your musical expression and creativity. Here's how to get started with the pentatonic scales on the ukulele:

What Are Pentatonic Scales?

1. **Definition:** Pentatonic scales consist of five notes per octave, eliminating some of the half-step intervals found in seven-note scales.

This simplicity makes them easier to play and less likely to produce dissonant sounds.

2. Types: The two most common types are the major pentatonic scale and the minor pentatonic scale.

Each has its own unique sound and application. Making them a great addition to your arsenal of scales.

The Major Pentatonic Scale

1. **Structure:** The major pentatonic scale is derived from the major scale by omitting the fourth and seventh degrees.

The pattern is: 1st, 2nd, 3rd, 5th, and 6th notes.

2. **C Major Pentatonic Example:** On the ukulele, the C major pentatonic scale can be played as follows:

C Major Scale: C D E F G A B = 1 2 3 4 5 6 7

C Major Pentatonic: C D E G A = 1 2 3 5 6

This scale has a pleasant, cheerful, uplifting sound that is ideal for creating joyful, melodic solos.

The Minor Pentatonic Scale

1. **Structure:** The minor pentatonic scale is derived from the natural minor scale, omitting the second and sixth degrees.

The pattern is: 1st, 3rd, 4th, 5th, and 7th notes.

2. **A Minor Pentatonic Example:** On the ukulele, the A minor pentatonic scale can be played as follows:

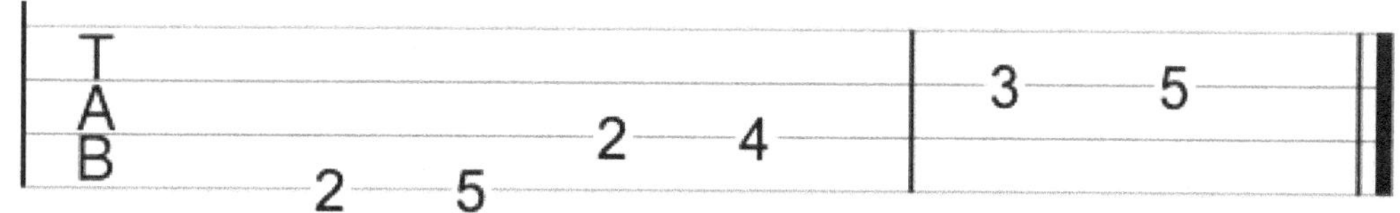

A Minor Scale: A B C D E F G = 1 2 b3 4 5 b6 b7

A Minor Pentatonic: A C D E G = 1 b3 4 5 b7

This scale has a soulful, bluesy sound and is often used in genres like rock and blues for its expressive qualities.

Practicing Pentatonic Scales

1. **Finger Exercises:** Practice playing the pentatonic scales daily to firmly establish them in memory.

Focus on clean transitions and maintaining a steady rhythm.

2. **Improvisation:** Use the pentatonic scales as a foundation for improvisation.

Experiment with creating melodies and solos over backing tracks or chord progressions.

3. **Integration:** Incorporate pentatonic scales into your practice routine by using them in various musical contexts, such as playing along with songs or composing your own pieces.

By mastering the pentatonic scales, you'll expand your musical vocabulary and gain the ability to create expressive solos and melodies on the ukulele. These scales are an essential tool for any musician looking to enhance their improvisational skills and explore new musical horizons.

Chapter V Quiz

In Chapter 5, you learn about playing scales. This involves developing finger dexterity, major and minor scales, and the pentatonic scale. All are crucial for playing melody.

Q: What is beneficial about the spider walk exercise?
A: ____

Q: How can a metronome benefit developing finger dexterity?
A: ____

Q: What is the whole step formula for the major scale?
A: ____

Q: What is the whole step formula for the minor scale?
A: ____

Q: What notes are altered in a major scale to make it a minor?
A: ____

Q: How many notes are in the minor pentatonic scale?
A: ____

Chapter V Summary

First, you learn that developing finger dexterity is crucial for ukulele players who want to play with precision and fluidity. This skill allows you to navigate the fretboard and perform intricate melodies.

Second, you learn that using open strings and changing up the order allows different fingers to lead the exercise. This helps with improving finger independence, muscle memory, and eye-hand coordination.

Third, you learn that major and minor scales are essential for any ukulele player looking to expand their musical knowledge and enhance their playing skills. These scales form the foundation and are crucial for musical development.

Fourth, you learn about how the minor scale is created by altering three notes of the major scale. The third, sixth, and 7th notes. These are flattened by a half step to create a sad, somber sound that contrasts with the major's bright sound.

Lastly, you learn about the major and minor pentatonic scales. These are created using only five notes from the major and minor scales, making them easier to learn and use.

Chapter VI: Playing Fingerstyle

Lesson 16: Fingerpicking Patterns

Fingerpicking introduces a dynamic layer to your ukulele playing, moving beyond simple strumming. By mastering various fingerpicking patterns, you can create intricate musical textures and explore new styles.

Understanding Fingerpicking Basics

1. Hand Position: Position your right hand over the sound hole, keeping your fingers slightly curved.

Your thumb should manage the G and C strings, while your index and middle fingers handle the E and A strings, respectively.

2. **Finger Labels:** In fingerpicking notation, the thumb is labeled "P," the index finger "I," the middle finger "M," and the ring finger "A."

Basic Fingerpicking Patterns

1. **Thumb-Index-Middle (P-I-M):** Pluck the G string with your thumb (P), the C string with your index finger (I), and the E string with your middle finger (M).

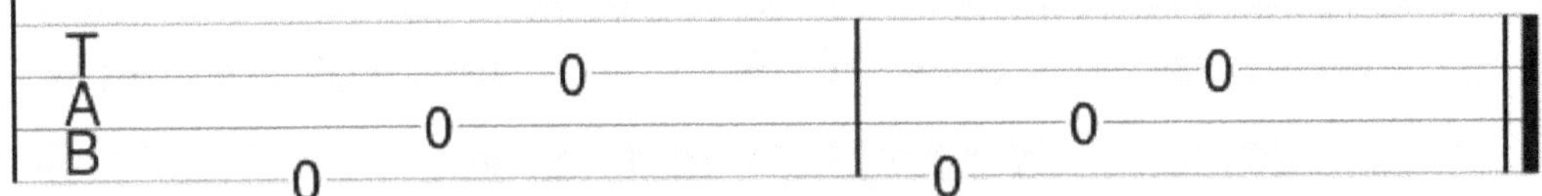

2. **Thumb-Index-Middle-Index (P-I-M-I):** Pluck the G string with your thumb (P), the C string with your index finger (I), the E string with your middle finger (M), and return to the C string with your index finger (I).

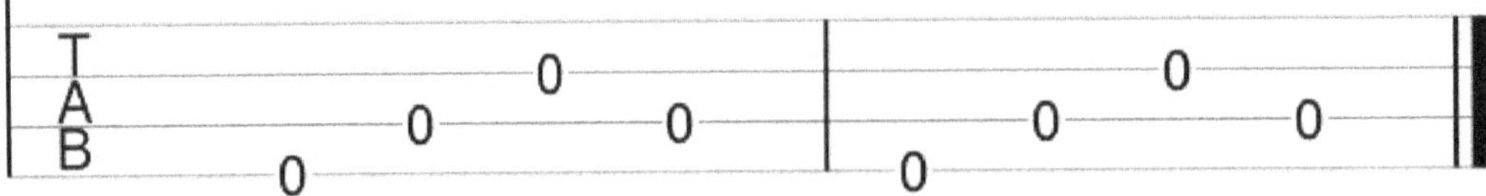

3. Travis Picking (P-I-M-A): Pluck the G string with your thumb (P), the C string with your index finger (I), the E string with your middle finger (M), and the A string with your ring finger (A).

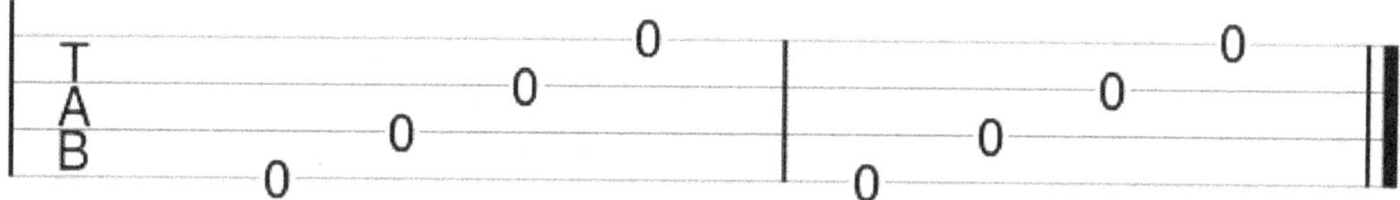

Additional Fingerpicking Patterns

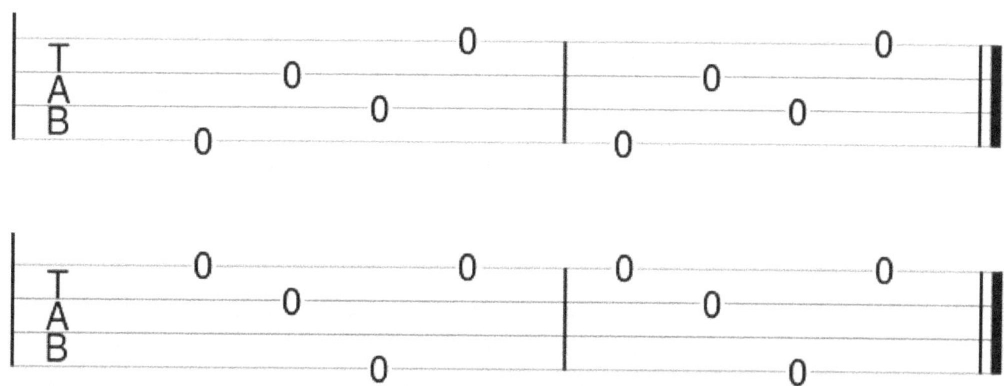

Work on these daily to improve your finger dexterity, control, and thumb use. This will lay the foundation for playing fingerpicking-style songs.

Practice Tips

1. **Start Slow:** Begin each pattern slowly to ensure accuracy.

Gradually increase speed as you gain confidence.

2. **Use a Metronome:** Practicing with a metronome will help you maintain a steady rhythm.

It will also help you increase your speed and accuracy.

3. **Practice Daily:** Apply these patterns consistently for maximum effectiveness.

Applying this technique daily will help you develop finger muscle memory for smoother playing.

4. **Incorporate with Chords**: Using the thumb and fingers to play individual notes within chords.

This will help you to choose an alternate approach to playing chords. Different from strumming.

Lesson 17: Fingerpicking Arpeggios

Arpeggios are a beautiful way to explore fingerstyle playing, allowing you to play chords in a broken, melodious manner. This technique is essential for creating rich, flowing musical passages on the ukulele.

What Are Arpeggios?

1. **Definition:** An arpeggio involves playing the notes of a chord sequentially rather than simultaneously.

This creates a cascading effect that adds depth and an emotional feel to your music.

2. **Applications:** Arpeggios are used in various musical genres, including classical, folk, and pop.

This adds dynamics and complexity to your musical compositions.

Practicing Arpeggios

1. **Simple Arpeggio Pattern:** Start with a basic pattern such as P-I-M-A, plucking the strings sequentially from G to A.

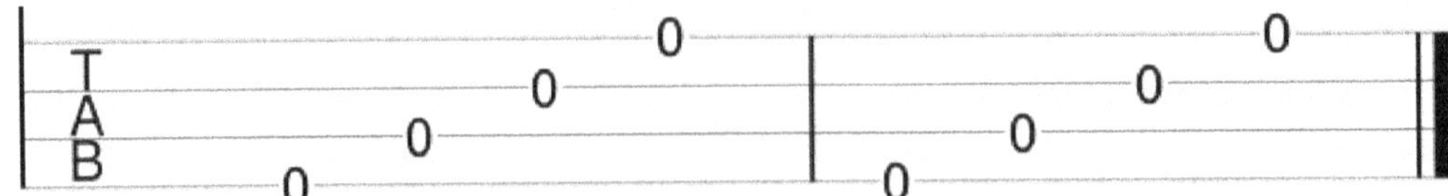

2. **Chord-Based Arpeggios:** Choose a chord, such as C major, and practice arpeggiating it using a simple pattern.

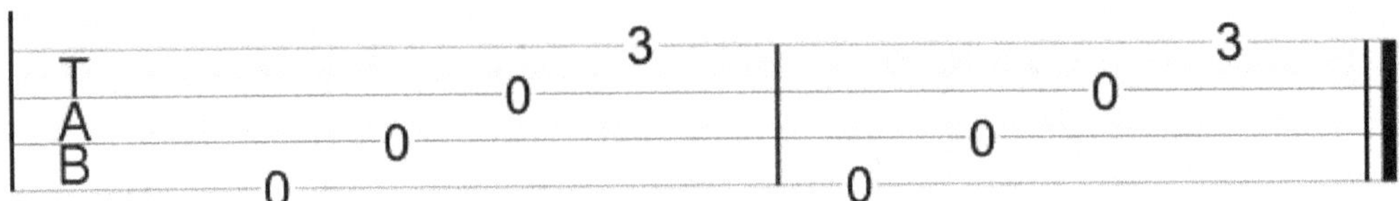

3. **Ascending and Descending:** Practice playing arpeggios in both directions to develop fluidity and control.

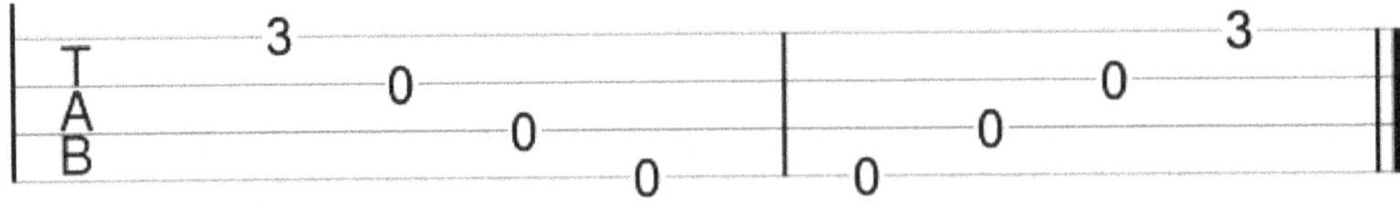

Additional Ukulele Arpeggios

G Major Arpeggio: G B D

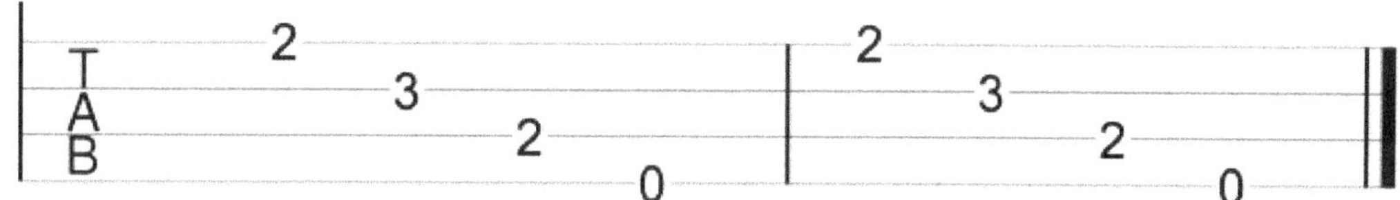

F Major Arpeggio: F A C

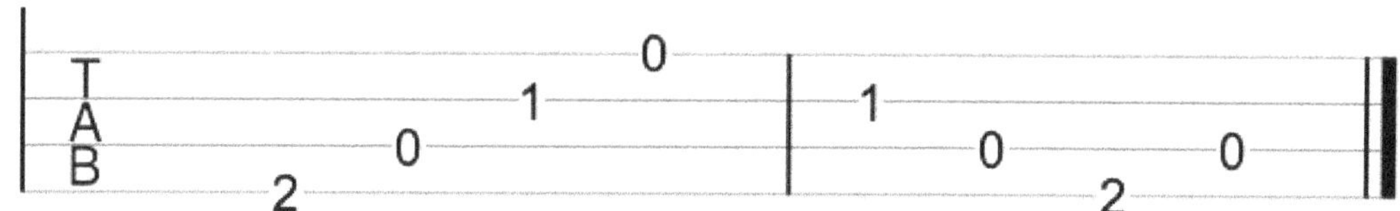

A Minor Arpeggio: A C E

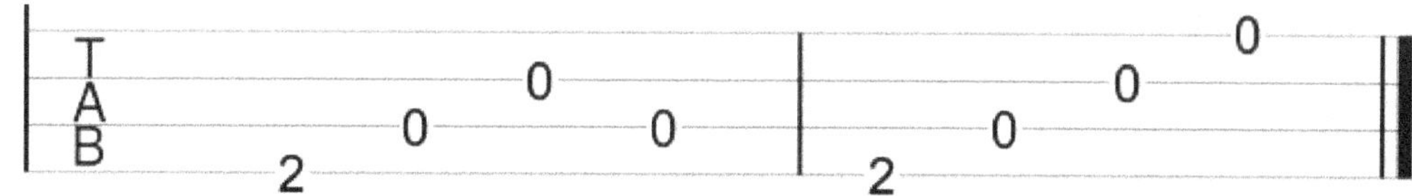

E Minor Arpeggio: E G B

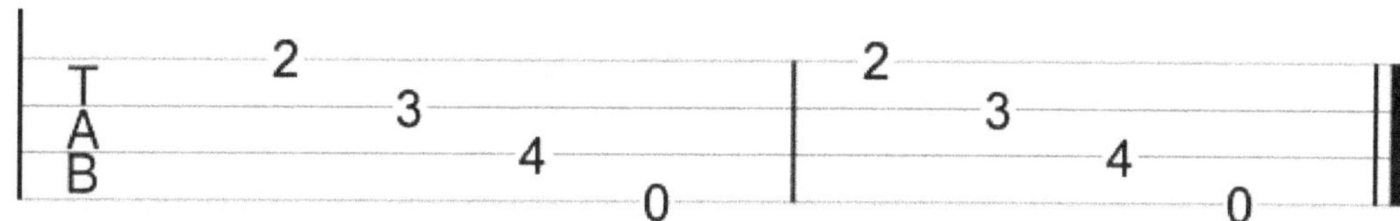

D Major Arpeggio: D F# A

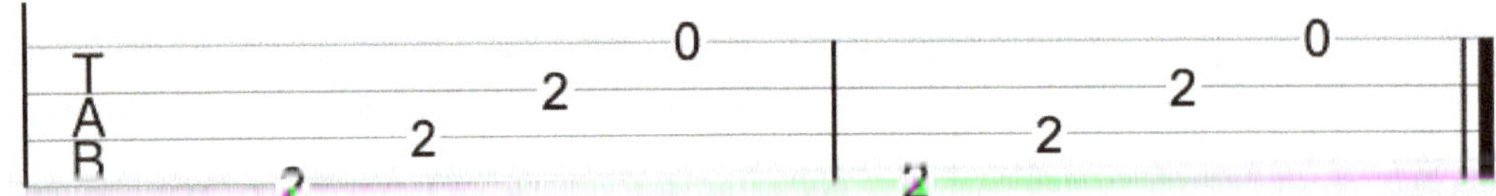

C and F Major Arpeggio: C E G and F A C

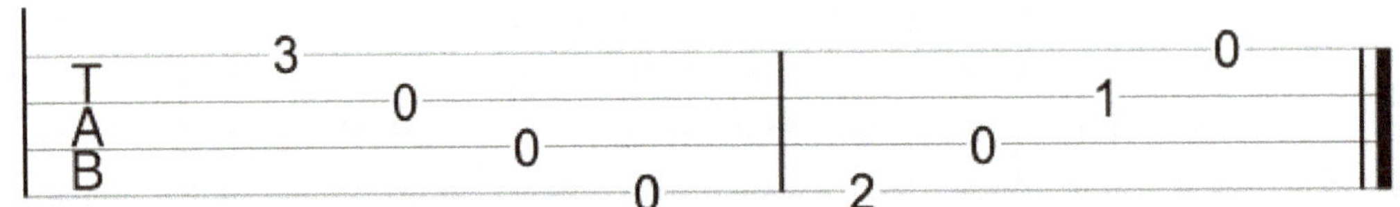

F Major and G7 Arpeggio: F A C and G B D F

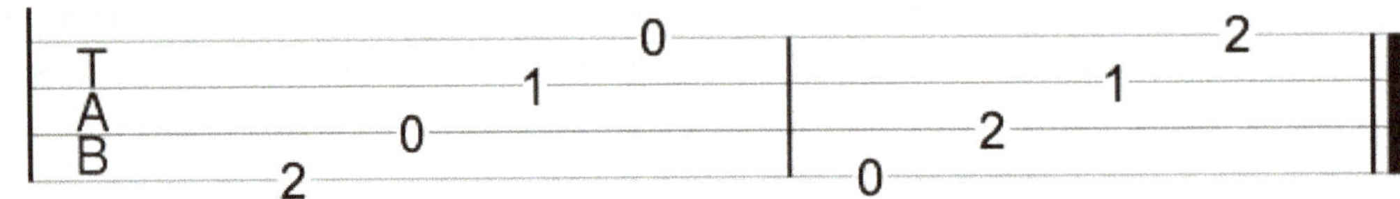

G7 and C Major Arpeggio: G B D F and C E G

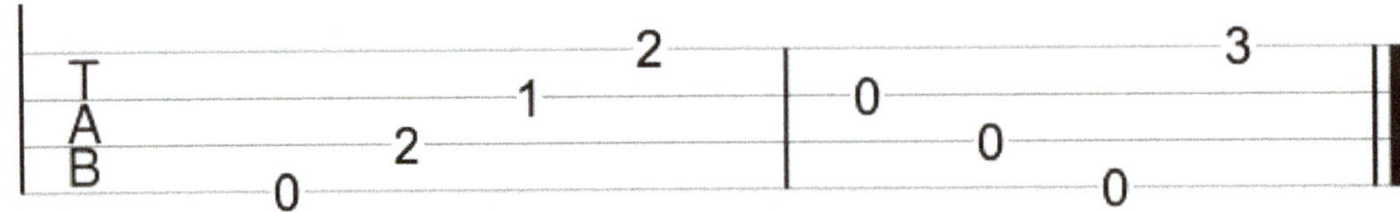

Tips for Mastery

1. Focus on Clarity: Ensure each note rings clearly and cleanly.

Pay attention to finger placement, string pressure, and play on the tips of your fingers.

2. Experiment with Speed: Start slowly, then gradually increase your speed.

This will allow you to maintain accuracy and develop fluidity in your playing.

3. Incorporate Dynamics: Experiment with dynamics, varying the volume and intensity of your picking to add expression.

These shape a song's structure and maintain the listener's interest.

Enhance your musicianship and playability by focusing on these aspects of musical development daily for optimum outcome.

Lesson 18: Fingerstyle and Strumming

Integrating fingerstyle with strumming allows you to create dynamic and varied musical pieces on the ukulele. This lesson will guide you through toohniquoo to ocamlcssly blend these styles, enhancing your musical versatility.

Transitioning Between Techniques

1. **Smooth Transitions:** Practice transitioning between strumming and fingerpicking within a couple of chords.

Start with simple chords and gradually increase complexity.

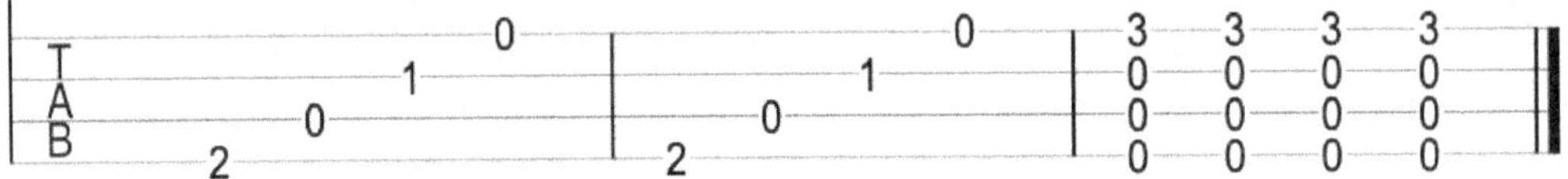

In this example, you arpeggiate an F major chord for two measures, and strum a C major chord for one measure.

2. Timing and Rhythm: Use a metronome to help with timing.

This approach will ensure smooth transitions between techniques.

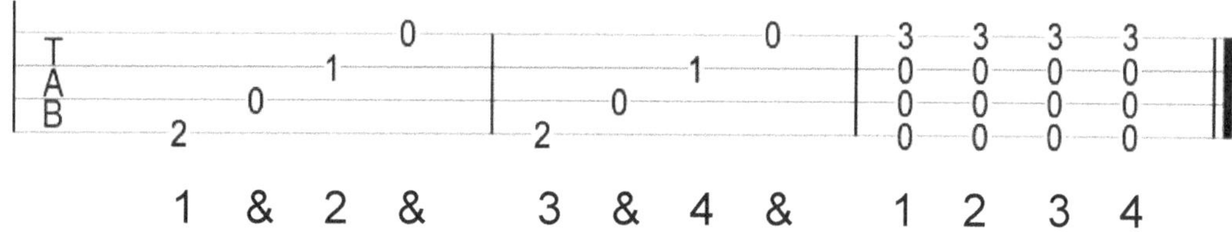

Notice how the timing sequence has you arpeggiate the F major faster than you strum the C major chord in the last measure.

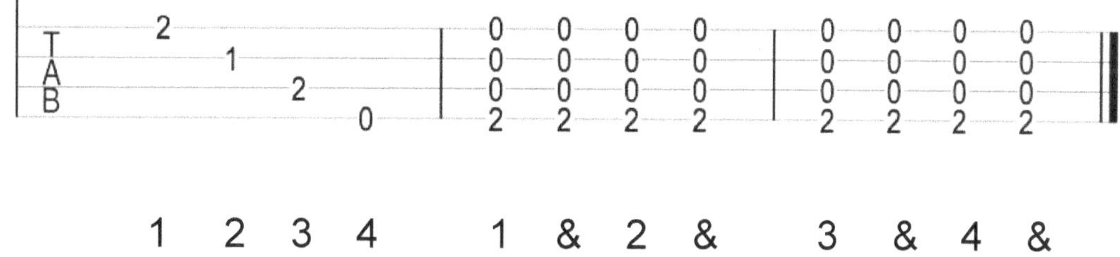

In this example, you arpeggiate the G7 chord for the first measure, and strum the A minor for the next two. Notice hw the timing sequence has been reversed.

Experiment with different chords and timing sequences.

Tips for Blending Techniques

1. **Strum-Pick Patterns:** Develop patterns that combine strumming with fingerpicking.

Such as starting with a strum and moving into a fingerpicked passage.

2. **Dynamic Variation:** Use strumming for more energetic sections and fingerpicking for softer, more intricate parts.

This allows you to create contrast and control of emotion within your musical landscapes.

3. **Claw Method:** Use your thumb on the G string, your fingers on the A and E strings, pluck them at the same time.

This will create a distinctive rhythm unlike picking the strings individually.

By combining fingerstyle and strumming, dynamic variations, and the claw method, you open up your playing to a much wider range of self-expression within a musical context.

More Fingerstyle and Strumming Examples

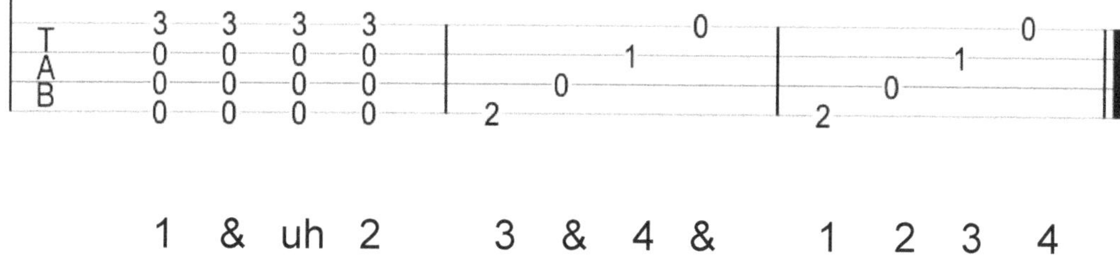

In this example, you strum the C major chord with a triplet and quarter note, and then arpeggiate the F major with an eighth and quarter note sequence over two measures.

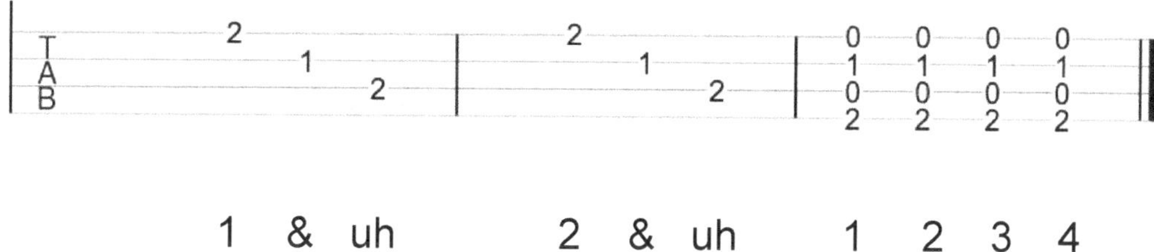

In this example, you arpeggiate the G7 chord with a triplet sequence for two measures, and then strum the F major chord with quarter notes for one measure.

As you can see, by mastering the timing sequences learned previously, quarter, eighth, triplet, etc, you can craft out different rhythms while using a few different chords.

Practice Tips

1. **Experiment with Songs:** Choose songs that incorporate both techniques and practice blending them naturally.

This will help you gain insight into these techniques so you can use them in your own songwriting.

2. **Focus on Expression:** Use these techniques to express different emotions and moods within your music.

Another reason for learning to play your favorite songs. They fuel your creativity with ideas and musical concepts.

3. **Daily Application:** Apply these techniques daily for maximum efficiency.

This will build finger dexterity and muscle memory in your thumb and fingers, improving your playing stamina.

By mastering the combination of strumming and fingerpicking, you'll expand your musical repertoire and enhance your ability to express a wide range of musical ideas on the ukulele.

Chapter VI Quiz

In Chapter 6, you have learned about playing fingerstyle. This includes learning fingerpicking patterns, learning fingerpicking arpeggios, and combining strumming with fingerstyle.

Q: What finger is commonly used to pluck the A string?
A: ____

Q: What is known as the Travis picking pattern fingerstyle?
A: ____

Q: What is a fingerstyle arpeggio in playing the ukulele?
A: ____

Q: Why is the benefit of practicing arpeggios on the ukulele?
A: ____

Q: What is the benefit of combining fingerstyle with strumming?
A: ____

Q: How can you create contrast by using these techniques?
A: ____

*Remember, the answers will be within the lessons.

Chapter VI Summary

First, you learn how fingerpicking introduces a dynamic layer to your ukulele playing, moving beyond simple strumming. By mastering various fingerpicking patterns, you can create intricate musical textures and explore new styles.

Second, you learn about fingerpicking basics. Using the thumb to pluck the G string while the index, middle, and ring fingers are used for the C, E, and A strings. This technique is developed through fingerpicking patterns.

Third, you learn that arpeggios are a beautiful way to explore fingerstyle playing, allowing you to play chords in a broken, melodious manner. This technique is essential for creating rich, flowing musical passages on the ukulele.

Fourth, you learn that an arpeggio involves playing the notes of a chord sequentially rather than simultaneously. This creates a cascading effect that adds depth and an emotional feel to your music.

Lastly, you learn that integrating fingerstyle with strumming allows you to create dynamic and varied musical pieces on the ukulele. Seamlessly blending these styles will enhance your musical versatility.

Chapter VII: Basic Music Theory

Lesson 19: Basic Chord Theory

Understanding music theory is fundamental for any musician, including ukulele players. It provides a framework for how music works. Chords are the building blocks of music, and understanding their structure is essential for playing and composing on the ukulele. Here's an introduction to the basics of chord theory:

What is a Chord?

- **Definition:** A chord is a combination of three or more notes played simultaneously.

Chords provide harmony and depth to music.

- **Triads:** The most basic chord structure is the triad, consisting of three notes: the root, third, and fifth.

For example, a C major triad includes the notes C, E, and G.

Types of Chords

- **Major chords:** These often sound happy and bright. They consist of a root, a major third, and a perfect fifth.

G Major: G B D = 1 3 5

D Major: D F# A = 1 3 5

A Major: A C# E = 1 3 5

E Major: E G# B = 1 3 5

- **Minor Chords:** Typically sound sad or somber. They consist of a root, a minor third, and a perfect fifth.

A Minor: A C E = 1 b3 5

B Minor: B D E = 1 b3 5

D Minor: D F A = 1 b3 5

E Minor: E G B = 1 b3 5

Remember, the minor triad will always have a flattened or minor third in it. So, to turn a major into a minor, alter the third note.

- **Seventh Chords:** Add an extra note to create a richer sound. Common types include major sevenths and dominant sevenths.

CM7: C E G B = 1 3 5 7 (Major with a natural 7th)

C7: C E G Bb = 1 3 5 b7 (Major with a flattened 7th)

GM7: G B D A# = 1 3 5 7 (Major with a natural 7th)

G7: G B D A = 1 3 5 b7 (Major with a flattened 7th)

AM7: A C# E G# = 1 3 5 7 (Major with a natural 7th)

A7: A C# E G = 1 3 5 b7 (Major with e flattened 7th)

The seventh chords are unique in the fact that they create a very distinct sound. Especially the dominant seventh chords. These will be noted by just the letter and number, as in G7.

By adding a flattened seventh note to the major triad (1, 3, 5), you create a chord that is very popular in many songs.

The 12 Notes of the Musical Alphabet

A A# B C C# D D# E F F# G G#

1   2   3 4   5   6   7   8 9 10 11 12

These twelve notes are what make up all the chords and scales that you will encounter when playing the ukulele, or any other instrument in Western Music.

These provide the roots of your musical vocabulary. So you want to make sure to spend some time memorizing them to master all your chords and scales.

Notes along the Ukulele Fretboard

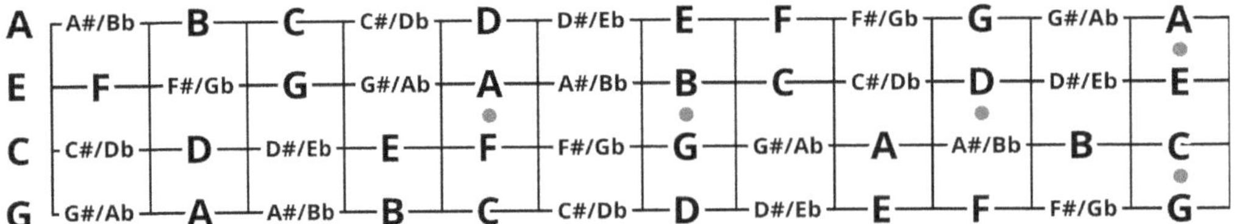

As you can see from this diagram, all twelve notes reside on each string of the ukulele. They also follow the same order. Master your notes, and you'll master the fretboard.

Building Chords on the Ukulele

- **Root Position:** The root note is the lowest note in the chord, and establishes the chord foundation.

Learn to identify and play chords in root position. These are the ones taught earlier. C, F, G, etc.

- **Inversions:** Change the order of notes in a chord to create different voicings. This will allow for different textures.

Whenever the 3rd or 5th of the triad is the lowest note, this creates an inversion and a different shade of color.

- **Practice:** Start with basic major and minor chords, then explore sevenths and inversions.

By starting with the major and minor triads and building out from there, you develop a deeper understanding of chord theory and chord construction.

Lesson 20: Basic Scale Theory

Scales are the foundation of melody and harmony. Scales go well with chords, because the chords are derived from scales. Understanding scales helps you to not only navigate the fretboard and compose music, but also understand chords better.

What is a Scale?

- **Definition:** A scale is a sequence of notes in a specific order of whole and half steps, like the major scale.

Scales are used to create melodies and harmonize music as well as determine chord voicings.

- **Major and Minor Scales:** These are the most common types of scales.

The major scale sounds bright and happy, while the minor scale sounds sad and somber.

You want to remember this about these scales, as they allow you to direct the emotion of the song structure.

Understanding Scale Construction

- **Whole and Half Steps:** The major scale pattern is W-W-H-W-W-W-H. The minor scale pattern is W-H-W-W-H-W-W.

C Major: C-w-D-w-E-h-F-w-G-w-A-w-B-h-C

A Minor: A-w-B-h-C-w-D-w-E-h-F-w-G-w-A

These scientific formulas are "magical" in the fact that they allow you to know all notes within any major or minor key. Just memorize the whole step, half-step sequence, and you will be correct every time.

This is the science and math of music. Music theory can be reduced to mathematical numbers and scientific formulas. Once you grasp this concept, it will make learning and understanding it easier.

Scales to Practice on the Ukulele

The C Major Scale: 1 2 3 4 5 6 7

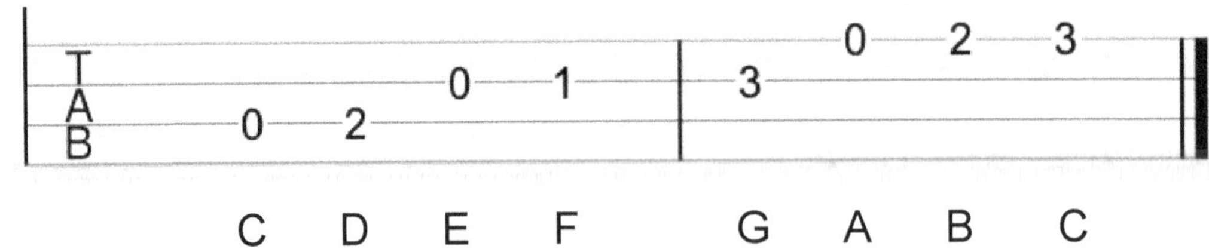

The C Major Pentatonic Scale: 1 2 3 5 6

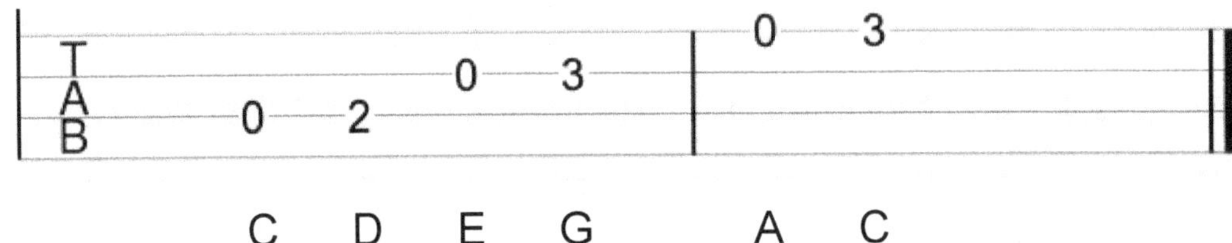

The A Natural Minor Scale: 1 2 b3 4 5 b6 b7

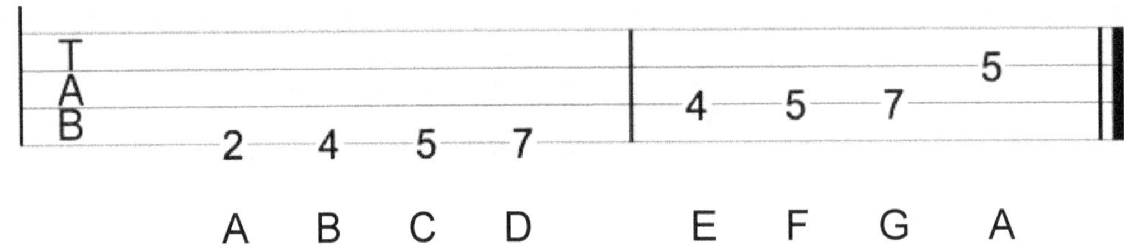

The A Minor Pentatonic Scale: 1 b3 4 5 b7

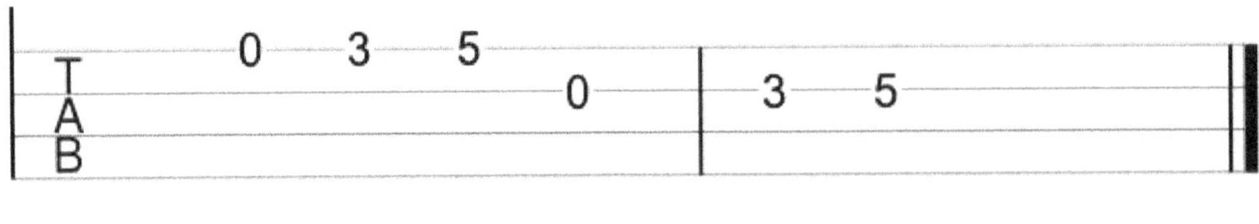

Tips For Practicing Scales on the Ukulele

- **Fretboard Familiarity:** Practice scales up and down the fretboard to become comfortable with different positions.

Listen to how the same notes vary in tone on different strings, and along different parts of the fretboard.

- **Speed and Precision:** Start slowly to ensure accuracy, then increase speed as you become more confident.

This is where the metronome can help. It can help you to build speed and stay on tempo as you do.

- **Integration:** Use scales in improvisation and melody creation to enhance your musical expression.

Increase your knowledge of each scale's tone and pattern across the fretboard. This will allow you to choose the right one to convey the emotion you want.

Lesson 21: Majors and Relative Minors

Understanding the relationship between major and minor scales is crucial for musicians aiming to deepen their grasp of music theory and enhance their musical creativity.

Major and Relative Minor Keys

What Are Relative Minor Keys?

- **Definition:** Every major key has a relative minor key that shares the same key signature.

This means that they contain the same notes but start on different root notes.

- **Relationship:** The relative minor is located three half steps (or a minor third) below the major key.

For example, the relative minor of C major is A minor.

C Major: C D E F G A B = 1 2 3 4 5 6 7

A Minor: A B C D E F G = 1 2 b3 4 5 b6 b7

Identifying Relative Minor Keys

- **Tonal Center:** While the notes are the same in each key, the tonal center of the key changes.

In the key of G major, the tonal center is G, whereas in E minor, it is E. Same as the C major, to A minor.

- **Example:** G Major and E minor share the same notes, like C major and A minor do. But they differ in emotional quality due to their tonal centers.

G Major: G A B C D E F# = 1 2 3 4 5 6 7

E Minor: E F# G A B C D = 1 2 b3 4 5 b6 b7

If you look at the E major, you have four sharpened notes: the F#, G#, C#, and D#. By flattening the 3rd, 6th, and 7th notes, you create the natural minor scale.

As you can see, this scale is made up of the same notes as the G major scale, which is what makes them relative.

Remember, every major has a relative minor.

Practicing Tips

C Major and A Minor

- **C Major Scale:** Play the C major scale starting from the open C string and using the sequence of C, D, E, F, G, A, B, and back to C.

This will help you to know this scale along the fretboard. Once you learn your notes, you can play them in multiple places.

- **A Minor Scale:** Begin on the A string and follow the note sequence A, B, C, D, E, F, G, and back to A.

Exploring the D major, B minor.

- **D Major and B Minor:** Just like the other scales that we have looked at, the D major (D, E, F#, G, A, B, C#) relates to the B minor (B, C#, D, E, F#, G, A).

D major: D E F# G A B C# = 1 2 3 4 5 6 7

B Minor: B C# D E F# G A = 1 2 b3 4 5 b6 b7

As you can see, the relative minor is located at the 6th position.

Applications in Music

Songwriting and Composition

- **Mood and Emotion:** Utilize the major scale for brighter, more uplifting sections, and switch to the relative minor for more introspective or melancholic passages.

This concept can be applied to the verse, chorus, and bridge. To encompass broader instrumental and structural elements.

- **Chord Progressions:** Experiment with progressions that transition between major and relative minor chords to create dynamic musical narratives.

Major chords will provide a sense of stability, while minor chords will add a sad, somber quality that can create tension and contrast in the composition.

- **Strum and Fingerstyle:** By experimenting with both of these applications, you can transition between major and relative minor chords and add dynamic expression to your musical landscapes.

Tips For Improvisation

- **Melodic Exploration:** Use the shared notes of major and relative minor scales for improvisation.

This can help you create solos that transition smoothly between moods.

- **Chords within the scales:** Each note within the scales can produce a major or minor chord.

Major: 1 = M, 2 = m, 3 = m, 4 = M, 5 = M, 6 = m, and 7 = diminished.

The diminished triad has a flat 5th note. 1, b3, b5.

Minor: 1 = m, 2 = dim, 3 = M, 4 = m, 5 = m, 6 = M, 7 = M.

This formula works with all major and minor keys.

By understanding major and relative minor theory, you expand your musical toolkit, allowing you to create more nuanced and expressive music on the ukulele. This knowledge works for any musician looking to deepen their theoretical understanding and enhance their creative expression.

Chapter VII Quiz

In Chapter 7, you learned about basic music theory. This includes basic chord theory, basic scale theory, and major and relative minor theory.

Q: What characteristics make up a major chord triad?

A: ____

Q: What are the different characteristics of a minor triad?

A: ____

Q: What is the whole step pattern of the minor scale?

A: ____

Q: Why is practicing scales important for ukulele players?

A: ____

Q: What is it that C major and A minor are relative keys?

A: ____

Q: What are the major and minor chords in the key of G major?

A: ____

*Knowing the answers to these will enhance your musicianship.

Chapter VII Summary

<u>First</u>, you learn that understanding music theory provides a framework for how music works. Chords are the building blocks of music, and understanding their structure is essential for playing and composing on the ukulele.

<u>Second</u>, you learn that a chord is a combination of three or more notes played simultaneously. Chords provide harmony and depth to music. The most basic chord structure is the triad, consisting of three notes: the root, third, and fifth.

<u>Third</u>, you learn that scales are the foundation of melody and harmony. Scales go well with chords, because the chords are derived from scales. Understanding scales can help you navigate the fretboard and compose music better.

<u>Fourth</u>, you learn that scales are notes in a specific sequence and can be broken down into major and minor. The major scale sounds bright and happy, while the minor scale sounds sad and somber.

<u>Lastly</u>, you learn that every major key has a relative minor. This is a minor key composed of the same notes. This allows you to move between the two seamlessly while providing contrast in your music.

Chapter VIII: Additional Training

Lesson 22: Setting Guitar Goals

Setting clear and achievable goals is an essential part of any learning journey, including mastering the ukulele. By establishing goals, you can track your progress, maintain motivation, and ensure continuous improvement. Here's a guide to help you set effective goals for your ukulele practice:

Understanding the Importance of Goal Setting

1. Direction and Focus: Goals provide a clear path for your practice sessions.

This can help you focus on the specific areas you want to improve in.

2. Motivation: Having tangible objectives can keep you motivated.

Particularly when you achieve milestones and see your progress.

3. **Measurement:** Goals help you track your progress and adjust your practice routine as needed.

This helps you achieve your aspirations and stay on target for where you need to be.

Types of Goals

1. **Short-Term Goals:** These are specific objectives you aim to achieve within a few days or weeks.

Examples include learning a new song, mastering a chord progression, or improving strumming techniques.

2. **Medium-Term Goals:** Set for one to three months, these goals might involve performing a piece at a local open mic.

Or possibly participating in a ukulele workshop, or expanding your song repertoire.

3. **Long-Term Goals:** These encompass broader aspirations such as becoming proficient in fingerstyle playing, composing original music, or joining a band.

All these things will take time to develop. That is why they are on the long-term goal list.

Setting SMART Goals

1. **Specific:** Clearly define what you want to achieve. Instead of "get better at ukulele," set a goal like "learn to play 'Somewhere Over the Rainbow' accurately."

This will give your mind focus and set you on a clear course of action.

2. **Measurable:** Ensure your goal can be quantified. For instance, "practice scales for 15 minutes daily" is measurable.

This allows you to stay steady and make the most of your practice time.

3. **Achievable:** Set realistic goals based on your current skill level. Challenge yourself, but avoid setting goals that are too far beyond your reach.

If you set goals that are too far beyond your reach, you will have a hard time staying motivated to achieve them.

4. **Relevant:** Align your goals with your personal interests and musical aspirations.

If you love folk music, focus on goals that enhance your ability to play that genre.

5. **Time-Bound:** Set a deadline to achieve your goal and maintain focus and urgency.

For example, "master this song within two weeks." This keeps you on track and ensures you are doing what is necessary on a daily basis.

S.M.A.R.T goals are a great way to cover all the basics needed to get to the next level in your playing. Be sure they are used in setting goals.

Reviewing and Reflecting

1. **Regular Check-Ins:** Periodically review your goals to assess your progress and make any needed changes.

Many things in life can distract you. Regular check-ins help you stay on point.

2. **Reflect on Successes and Challenges:** Consider what strategies worked well and where you faced difficulties.

Celebrate your victories and double down on techniques and concepts you might struggle with.

By setting thoughtful and deliberate goals, you'll create a structured path to follow as you learn and grow as a ukulele player.

This approach will not only enhance your skills but also deepen your enjoyment and satisfaction from playing music.

Lesson 23: Developing Practice Habits

Developing effective practice habits is crucial for any musician striving to improve their skills and enjoy their musical journey. Consistent practice not only enhances your playing ability but also builds confidence and discipline. Here are some strategies to help you cultivate productive practice habits for the ukulele:

Benefits of Good Practice Habits

1. **Skill Development:** Regular practice leads to gradual improvement in technique, timing, and musicality.

Focus on small, manageable actions to build momentum and keep you motivated.

2. **Build Self-Confidence:** As you become more proficient, your confidence in playing the ukulele will naturally increase.

This will encourage you to tackle more challenging pieces and feel good about doing it.

3. **Discipline and Routine:** Establishing a dedicated practice routine fosters discipline.

This can benefit not only your musical proficiency but also other areas of your life.

Strategies for Development

Set Clear Goals

Although these were mentioned previously, it is important to fully grasp the significance of this skill-building concept.

- **Daily Objectives:** Identify specific goals for each practice session.

Such as mastering a particular chord transition or improving fingerpicking speed.

- **Long-Term Vision:** Keep your broader musical aspirations in mind to maintain motivation and direction.

Remember the reason why you want to learn. Performance, share knowledge, etc. This will keep your eye on the prize.

Create a Consistent Schedule

- **Regular Practice Time:** Set aside a specific time each day for practice.

This will help improve your performance, boost your memory, and provide a sense of control and stability.

- **Short, Focused Sessions:** Aim for 20–30-minute practice sessions, especially if you're just starting.

This helps maintain consistency in development, builds concentration, and prevents burnout.

- **Same Time Same Place:** Set aside a specific time each day for practice.

This will ensure your mind and body are focused on studying and practicing your instrument. Keeping you disciplined and motivated.

Resources, Tools, and Challenges

- **Metronome and Tuner:** Incorporate a metronome to enhance timing and a tuner to ensure accurate pitch.

These two tools alone will allow you to progress by leaps and bounds. Make sure to acquire and use them.

- **Instructional Materials:** Utilize online tutorials, books, or courses.

These will guide your practice sessions and introduce new concepts.

- **Dealing with Challenges:** Along your road to proficiency, you will encounter challenges.

During these times, focus more, put in more effort, and break through barriers with discipline and perseverance.

By developing strong practice habits, you'll set yourself up for success in your ukulele journey. Consistent, mindful practice will lead to steady improvement, making your musical experience more rewarding and enjoyable.

Lesson 24: Continue Your Musical Journey

As you reach the end of this ukulele guide, it's important to remember that learning an instrument is a lifelong journey filled with exploration, creativity, and personal growth. Whether you're playing for fun, relaxation, or as a stepping stone to broader musical pursuits, continuing your musical journey is all about embracing new challenges and savoring the joy of making music.

Here's how you can keep progressing and enjoying your ukulele experience:

Embrace Lifelong Learning

1. **Explore New Genres and Styles:** Don't limit yourself to one type of music.

Experiment with different genres, such as jazz, blues, classical, or reggae, to broaden your musical horizons and discover new techniques.

2. **Learn Advanced Techniques:** As you become more confident in your playing.

Challenge yourself with advanced techniques such as chord inversions, harmonics, and complex fingerstyle patterns.

3. **Seek Further Education:** Consider taking lessons from a professional instructor.

Attend workshops or participate in online courses to deepen your understanding of music theory and ukulele skills.

Engage with the Music Community

1. **Join a Ukulele Group or Band:** Playing with others can enhance your skills and provide valuable feedback.

Look for local ukulele clubs or online communities to connect with fellow enthusiasts.

2. **Perform Live:** Share your music with others by performing at open mic nights, community events, or family gatherings to build self-confidence.

3. **Collaborate with Other Musicians:** Collaborating with other instrumentalists or vocalists can inspire creativity and lead to new musical projects.

It can also help you communicate musical ideas and concepts, furthering your understanding of music.

Stay Inspired and Motivated

1. **Listen to Inspiring Music:** Regularly listen to a wide variety of music to find inspiration and new ideas for your own playing.

Each player brings a unique quality to the instrument. Listen to them, and gain insights that can enrich your playing style.

2. **Reflect on Your Progress:** Take time to appreciate how far you've come in your musical journey.

Reflect on your achievements and set intentions for future growth. This will keep you focused and motivated to keep learning new concepts and techniques.

3. **Keep a Music Journal:** Document your experiences, challenges, and successes in a music journal.

Revisiting your entries can help you see exactly where you are on your journey. This will motivate you and spark new ideas.

Set New Goals

1. **Personal Projects:** Start a new musical project, such as recording a cover album.

Composing original songs or creating a music video can spark new ideas that lead to expanded inspiration.

2. **Skill Mastery:** Identify a specific skill or technique you want to master and dedicate time to perfecting it.

If you'd like to be better at playing melody, expand your knowledge of scales, and if it's rhythm, expand your knowledge of chords.

3. **Cultural Exploration:** Learn about the cultural history of the ukulele and incorporate traditional Hawaiian songs into your repertoire.

Also, don't forget that most of your favorite contemporary songs you hear on the radio can be played on the ukulele. This aspect is what truly makes the instrument fun to learn.

By continuing to explore, learn, and connect with the musical world, you'll keep your ukulele journey vibrant and fulfilling.

Remember, the joy of playing music is as much about the journey as it is about the destination. Enjoy every note, every strum, and every new discovery along the way.

Chapter VIII Quiz

In Chapter 8, you learned about setting goals, developing practice habits, and what is needed to continue your musical journey.

Q: What is the purpose of setting goals for your playing?
A: ____

Q: How are S.M.A.R.T goals beneficial to your playing?
A; ____

Q: Why is it beneficial to have a consistent practice schedule?
A: ____

Q: What is a key component of a solid practice session?
A: ____

Q: How can the community enhance your ukulele proficiency?
A; ____

Q: What are ways you can stay motivated during your journey?
A: ____

Chapter VIII Summary

<u>First,</u> you learn that setting clear and achievable goals is an essential part of any learning journey, including mastering the ukulele. By establishing goals, you can track your progress, maintain motivation, and ensure continuous improvement.

<u>Second</u>, you learn that setting S.M.A.R.T goals is best. These are specific, measurable, achievable, relevant, and time-bound goals. These can also be broken down into short, medium, and long-term.

<u>Third</u>, you learn that developing effective practice habits is crucial for any musician striving to improve their skills and enjoy their musical journey. Consistent practice not only enhances your playing ability but also builds confidence and discipline.

<u>Fourth</u>, you learn that experimenting with different genres, such as jazz, blues, classical, or reggae, will broaden your musical horizons. Allowing you to discover new ukulele concepts and techniques.

<u>Lastly</u>, it's important to remember that learning an instrument is a lifelong journey filled with exploration, creativity, and personal achievement. Whether you're playing for fun or as a stepping stone to musical proficiency, it's best to keep growing.

Ukulele Mastery: Conclusion

Learning to play the ukulele is a rewarding journey that combines creativity, discipline, and a love for music. This guide has provided you with a comprehensive foundation, from the historical origins of the ukulele to practical skills such as holding the instrument, tuning, playing chords, and exploring advanced techniques like fingerstyle.

If you have gone through the lessons as they have been presented and practiced as recommended, you should have a solid grasp on the inner workings of understanding and playing the ukulele. For all your work, I say "Congratulations."

The ukulele's charm lies in its simplicity and versatility, making it an accessible instrument for musicians of all levels. Throughout your learning journey, remember that the ultimate goal is to enjoy the music you create. Embrace mistakes as learning opportunities and celebrate each milestone, no matter how small.

By continuously refining your technique and expanding your repertoire, you'll discover new ways to connect with the music and express your unique voice. The ukulele's vibrant sound has the power to bring joy not only to you but also to those who listen to your music.

As you continue to develop your skills, consider engaging with the broader musical community. Whether in a group setting or through collaborations, it can greatly enhance your learning experience. Sharing your progress and receiving feedback will help you grow as a musician.

Let this guide serve as a stepping stone towards a lifelong adventure filled with music, creativity, and personal fulfillment. Remember, every note you play contributes to your unique musical story, making your journey with the ukulele truly special.

To all your success,

Sincerely, Dwayne Jenkins

Other Books From Dwayne Jenkins

Learn Guitar Scale Theory:

Dive deep into guitar scale theory with this easy-to-learn, comprehensive guidebook. An understanding of theory can add a rich vocabulary for both harmony and melody.

Learning guitar scale theory will help you expand your improvisation skills, enhance your scale vocabulary, and deepen your understanding of intervals.

Demystifying the Blues Scales:

After mastering the pentatonic scales, I recommend you learn the blues scales. These utilize the "blue" note that allows you to expand your versatility in creating solos and melodies.

With step-by-step instructions, diagrams, notation, and exercises. All that will be needed is your desire to learn and time to practice. Explore the fun of playing the blues.

Learn Guitar Chord Theory:

If you'd like to learn more about chord theory and enhance your knowledge of chord construction, this book will do it. A great way to expand your guitar chord vocabulary.

Learn Guitar Chord Theory is a comprehensive study guide on the inner workings of guitar chords, with step-by-step lessons, diagrams, exercises, and learning assessments. All designed to unlock the mysteries of the fretboard.

All books are authored by Dwayne Jenkins, published by Tritone Publishing, and are available worldwide.

Digital formats of all titles are available for instant learning. Just download them to your computer and start learning anywhere, anytime.

Self-study is a great way to learn, as it allows you not only to go at your own pace but also to develop self-discipline and time management, which can benefit you in other areas of your life.

Also, check out Dwayne's Guitar Lessons video channel on YouTube. These are free lessons covering a wide range of guitar topics.

Whether you are working on rhythm, lead, theory, or guitar maintenance, it is all here in these lessons. These are available 24 hours a day, 7 days a week, 365 days a year.

If more help is needed, Dwayne also offers one-on-one coaching on his website.

www.DwaynesGuitarLessons.com

Best of luck, and be sure to have fun.

About the Author

Dwayne Jenkins is a guitar teacher with a unique, engaging approach that helps students of all ages and skill levels enjoy playing the guitar and ukulele. His enthusiasm and love for teaching shine through every lesson that he creates.

His lessons are designed to help you progress. No matter your reason for learning, there will always be something in Dwayne's books and products to help you achieve your dreams.

So if you're a student looking to start or a student looking to further your education, be sure to get involved with Dwayne's guitar lessons and learn what so many people have already discovered: why learning to play the guitar is one of the most incredible things you can do for yourself.

What Students Are Saying About Dwayne's Guitar Lessons

"Dwayne, thank you so much for everything you have taught me and done for me. You are an amazing guitarist and wonderful teacher". BJ.

"Dwayne, it has been a true pleasure to have you at our house each week! Ken & Trevor have learned so much through you and your teachings. Thank you!" Lisa.

"Dwayne, thank you for being a great teacher and teaching me many great songs. This is a skill that will last me a lifetime." Danielle.

"Dwayne, we want you to know we are honored to have you at the studio. We appreciate all that you do and are grateful that we can leave you in charge." Angie & Wilson M.E.C.

"Dwayne, we are so glad you are our Teacher. It's been three years already, can you believe it? Thank you again. You're the best!" Chelsey & Lucas.

"Dwayne, we are so glad that you are in our lives. Chelsey & Lucas enjoy their time with you and look up to you. Looking forward to another great year! Love and best wishes, Ken & Sue.

"Dwayne, thank you so much for being not only an awesome guitar teacher but an awesome friend as well," Kayla.

"Dwayne, thank you so much for all the years of doing lessons. You have been very patient with my progress, helped me build confidence, and inspired me to pursue my dreams. And in doing so, you have become a great friend." Jake.

"Dwayne, thank you for teaching Nick guitar so well. He loves it and is getting quite good, fast. I'm amazed!" Jane.

"Dwayne, thank you so much for teaching me every Saturday, and not only teaching me guitar but also about life, and helping me with setting my goals. You are a great teacher, mentor, and the best friend ever." Carson.

"There is no other person I would want to teach me a guitar! His 1-on-1 teaching makes learning guitar very personal & exhilarating. He teaches at your pace and takes pride in what "YOU" want to learn. The best part is that if Dwayne doesn't know a song a student wants to play, he takes time out of the week to learn it. His teaching comes to life in my performance and has progressed over the last 8 years. Words cannot describe how amazing a teacher, rockstar, and true friend Dwayne has become to me." Dominic.

Ukulele Resource Guide

Common Ukulele Chords

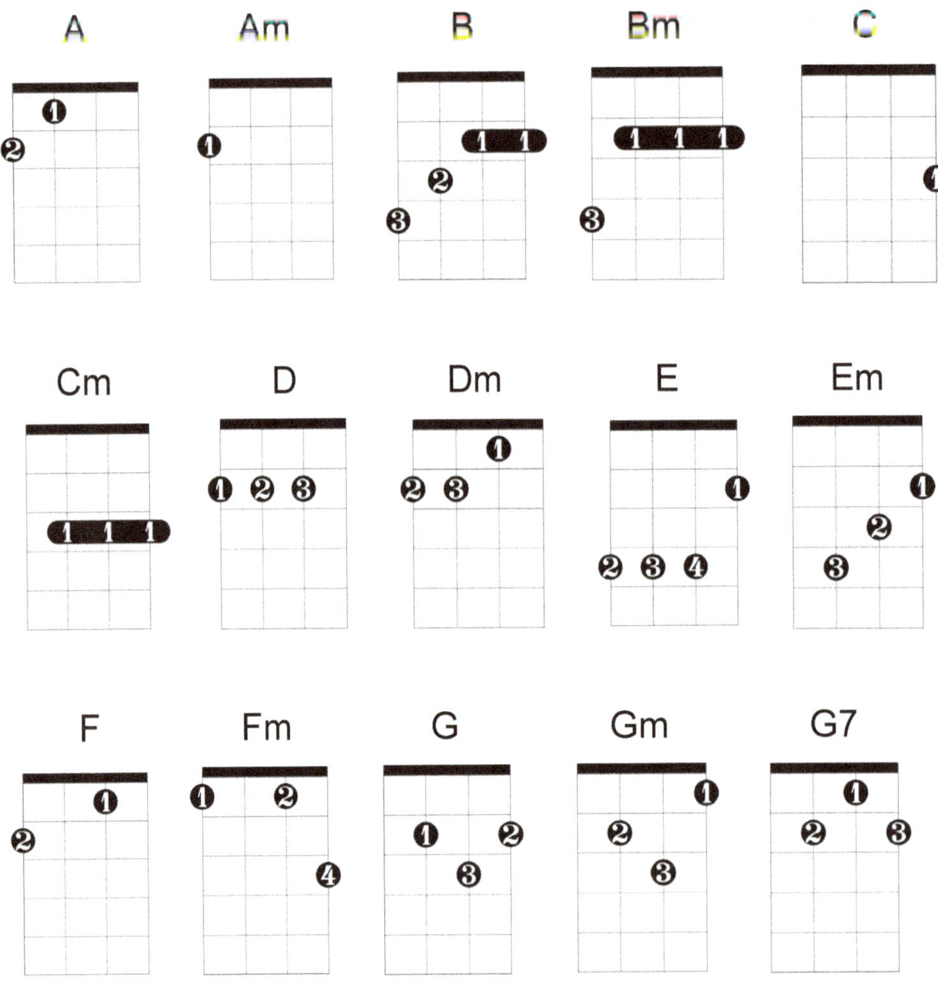

These are all chords found in many of your favorite songs.
Learn them and have them handy for when needed.

Resource Guide Continued

Basic Chord Theory: Chord formulas

Major Triad: 1 3 5	Minor Triad: 1 b3 5
Sus2 Triad: 1 2 5	Sus4 Triad: 1 4 5
Augmented Triad: 1 3 #5	Diminished Triad: 1 b3 b5
Major 6th: 1 3 5 6	Minor 6th: 1 3 5 6
Major 7th: 1 3 5 7	Minor 7th: 1 b3 5 b7
Dominant 7th: 1 3 5 b7	

Basic Scale Theory: Scale formulas

Major Scale: 1 2 3 4 5 6 7   Minor: 1 2 b3 4 5 b6 b7
Major Pentatonic: 1 2 3 5 6   Minor: 1 b3 4 5 b7

Relative Major Minor Theory: Two scales with the same notes

C Major: C D E F G A B = 1 2 3 4 5 6 7
A minor: A B C D E F G = 1 2 b3 4 5 b6 b7
G Major: G A B C D E F# = 1 2 3 4 5 6 7
E minor: E F# G A B C D = 1 2 b3 4 5 b6 b7
A Major: A B C# D E F# G# = 1 2 3 4 5 6 7
F# minor: F# G# A B C# D E = 1 2 b3 4 5 b6 b7
D Major: D E F# G A B C# = 1 2 3 4 5 6 7
B minor: B C# D E F# G A = 1 2 b3 4 5 b6 b7

Resource Guide Continued

The I-IV-V Chords in Multiple Keys

Key	I	IV	V
C	C	F	G
D	D	G	A
E	E	A	B
F	F	Bb	C
G	G	C	D
A	A	D	E
B	B	E	F#

This diagram shows you what chords will be best to use in these particular keys. These are the most common keys and chords that will be found in songs.

This makes an excellent quick reference guide. Remember, you can use the other chords within the key as well, but these are the ones I recommend you start with.

Experiment with these chords over the 12-bar blues progression. As you do so, your ear will become familiar with them, and you will hear how songs are constructed with them, which will give you ideas for constructing your own musical compositions.

Resource Guide Continued

Notes Within Common Major Keys: W-W-H-W-W-W-H

1. A Major: A B C# D E F# G# octave
2. B Major: B C# D# E F# G# A# octave
3. C Major: C D E F G A B octave
4. D Major: D E F# G A B C# octave
5. E Major: E F# G# A B C# D# octave
6. F Major: F G A Bb C D E octave
7. G Major: G A B C D E F# octave

Notes Within Common Minor Keys: W-H-W-W-H-W-W

1. A minor: A B C D E F G octave
2. B minor: B C# D E F# G A octave
3. C minor: C D Eb F G Ab Bb octave
4. D minor: A Bb C D E F G octave
5. E minor: E F# G A B C D octave
6. F minor: F G Ab Bb C Db Eb octave
7. G minor: G A Bb C D Eb F octave

Two Extra Common Minor Keys: W-H-W-W-H-W-W

1. B flat minor: Bb C Db Eb F Gb Ab
2. F sharp minor: F# G# A B C# D E

Notes